Marie-Antoinette

and the Petit Trianon at Versailles

FAÇADE du Chateau du coté du Jardin Francois.

COUPE du Chateau prise sur la ligne, A,B.

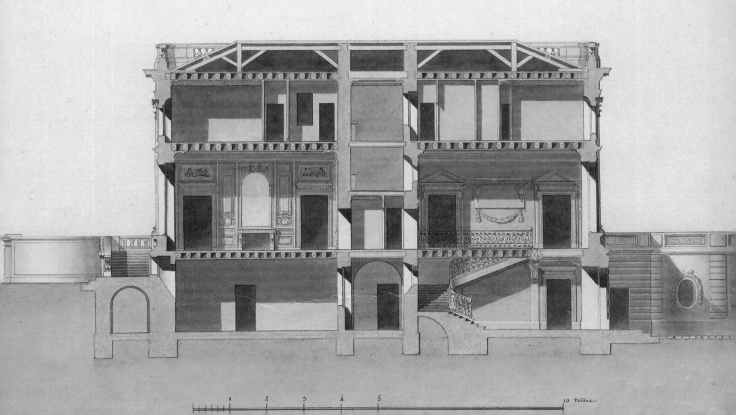

Marie-Antoinette
and the Petit Trianon at Versailles

Martin Chapman

Christian Baulez
Pierre-Xavier Hans
Alexandre Maral
Bertrand Rondot
Xavier Salmon

Fine Arts Museums of San Francisco
Etablissement public du musée et du domaine national de Versailles

Marie-Antoinette and the Petit Trianon at Versailles

Presented by

Bank of America

Fine Arts Museums of San Francisco, Legion of Honor
November 17, 2007–February 17, 2008

This exhibition is organized by the Fine Arts Museums of San Francisco in cooperation with the Etablissement public du musée et du domaine national de Versailles. The exhibition is also supported by the San Francisco Auxiliary of the Fine Arts Museums, Dr. Kathy Nicholson Hull and Mr. Bill Gisvold, Clare C. McEvoy Charitable Remainder Unitrust and Jay D. McEvoy Trust, George M. Bowles Trust, Hurlbut-Johnson Charitable Trusts, European Decorative Arts Council of the Fine Arts Museums, and Mr. and Mrs. Adolphus Andrews, Jr.

The catalogue is published with the assistance of the Andrew W. Mellon Foundation Endowment for Publications.

All objects with an inventory number prefixed by "Inv." are in the collection of the Musée du Château de Versailles.

Library of Congress Control Number: 2007935629

ISBN 978-0-88401-130-9

Marie-Antoinette and the Petit Trianon at Versailles was produced through the Publications Department of the Fine Arts Museums of San Francisco:

Ann Heath Karlstrom, Director of Publications and Graphic Design

Elisa Urbanelli, Managing Editor

"The History of the Petit Trianon" translated from the French by Rose Vekony

Catalogue entries (except those by Martin Chapman) translated from the French by Alexandra Bonfante-Warren

Front cover: Elisabeth Louise Vigée Le Brun (1755–1842), *Marie-Antoinette "à la rose,"* 1783 (cat. 16)
Back cover: Watercolor by Claude-Louis Châtelet (1750–1795), in *Souvenir Album of the Petit Trianon,* 1781 (cat. 63)
Page 2: Elevation and section of the Petit Trianon, in *Souvenir Album of the Petit Trianon,* 1781 (cat. 63)

Designed by Zach Hooker
Typeset by Brynn Warriner
Produced by Marquand Books, Inc., Seattle
    www.marquand.com
Color separations by iocolor, Seattle
Printed and bound in Canada

Contents

Foreword

The Fine Arts Museums of San Francisco and the Etablissement public du musée et du domaine national de Versailles are proud to collaborate in bringing the first-ever showing of works of art from the Petit Trianon to the United States. This event arises from the temporary closure of the château of the Petit Trianon in fall 2007 for a restoration made possible by the Société Montres Bréguet S.A. The result is a unique opportunity to appreciate, within the handsome neoclassical California Palace of the Legion of Honor, a number of famous pieces that have never before been loaned from their setting in Ange-Jacques Gabriel's often-imitated architectural masterpiece.

The Legion of Honor, one of the Fine Arts Museums of San Francisco, has had a long and distinguished involvement with the art and decorative arts of eighteenth-century France since its founding by Alma de Bretteville Spreckels in 1924. Mrs. Spreckels's generosity, as well as gifts made by her friends and associates from around the world, enriched the core collection. Among these gifts are a black lacquer commode by Martin Carlin probably made for Madame Du Barry, a grand garniture of *bleu fallot* Sèvres porcelain vases, and an elaborately decorated writing desk by Bernard II van Risenburgh, given by Archer M. Huntington. These are just part of a setting that provides an appropriate venue for this unique exhibition.

This display of paintings, sculpture, furniture, porcelain, prints, and drawings reflects the history of the Petit Trianon from its inception under Louis XV and Madame de Pompadour to its heyday under Marie-Antoinette, who transformed the estate into the magical pleasure ground that still fascinates and delights us today. It was here that the queen could avoid the glare of the public spotlight. At the Petit Trianon, hidden away in a far corner of the park at Versailles, Marie-Antoinette could lead a quiet, personal life where she said, "Je souhaiterais vivre à Trianon en personne particulière"—I wish to live at Trianon as a private person. The works of art from the Petit Trianon represent Marie-Antoinette's own interests and tastes. This wonderful array of objects assembled in San Francisco includes some of the contents of the Petit Trianon sold in 1793–1794 during the French Revolution. In 1867 Empress Eugénie inaugurated an exhibition on Marie-Antoinette at the Petit Trianon. Since that time this château has become home to objects associated with the former queen and a testament to the refined and elegant taste of the final years of the ancien régime.

We are most grateful to Jean-Jacques Aillagon, President of the Etablissement public du musée et du domaine national de Versailles, for his enthusiasm for this international cultural exchange. We particularly thank Martin Chapman, the Fine Arts Museums' curator of European decorative arts, who worked with the former curator of paintings at the Château de Versailles, Xavier Salmon, and with Pierre-Xavier Hans and Bertrand Rondot, current curators at Versailles, to bring together a marvelous group of objects that tell the story of Marie-Antoinette and the Petit Trianon. In a remarkably short time they have prepared an exhibition catalogue, the first devoted to this subject since Lescure's *Les Palais de Trianon* was published in association with the exhibition on Marie-Antoinette of 1867. We are also grateful to the officer in charge of exhibitions at Versailles, Hélène Flon, as well as to chief curator Christian Baulez and Alexandre Maral, curator of sculpture, for their assistance in bringing the exhibition and catalogue to fruition. Jean-Marc Manaï has provided much new photography for this project.

At the Fine Arts Museums, in addition to Martin Chapman, we thank Elisa Urbanelli for her exceptional work on producing this catalogue. We also thank Ann Karlstrom, Suzy Peterson, and Sue Grinols, as well as the photographers Joe McDonald and Jorge Bachman for their roles with the publication. Krista Brugnara, with Allison Satre, managed the exhibition logistics. Karin Breuer, with Anna Lucas, provided curatorial oversight for the works on paper. The beautiful exhibition design is indebted to Bill White and Elizabeth Scott, and the graphics to Juliana Pennington. Therese Chen and Karen Christenson handled registration, and Elisabeth Cornu and Debra Evans were responsible for conservation.

We would like to thank other lenders to the exhibition, including H.R.H. Moritz, Landgraf von Hessen, and H.R.H. Donatus, Prinz von Hessen; Mark Jones, Director of the Victoria and Albert Museum; Malcolm Rogers, Director of the Museum of Fine Arts, Boston; and the private collector whose loans have helped us round out the picture of Marie-Antoinette and the Petit Trianon.

It is a great privilege to recognize the presenting sponsor, Bank of America. We thank them for their continued support of the Fine Arts Museums and for their generosity and interest in this unique international project. We also extend thanks to the San Francisco Auxiliary of the Fine Arts Museums, Dr. Kathy Nicholson Hull and Mr. Bill Gisvold, Clare C. McEvoy Charitable Remainder Unitrust and Jay D. McEvoy Trust, George M. Bowles Trust, Hurlbut-Johnson Charitable Trusts, European Decorative Arts Council of the Fine Arts Museums, and Mr. and Mrs. Adolphus Andrews, Jr. The catalogue was produced with the assistance of the Andrew W. Mellon Foundation Endowment for Publications.

John E. Buchanan, Jr.
Director of Museums
Fine Arts Museums of San Francisco

Pierre Arizzoli-Clémentel
Directeur général du musée et
du domaine national de Versailles

Introduction:
The Legacy of the Petit Trianon in America

Martin Chapman

Americans have long admired the Petit Trianon for its simplicity, its noble proportions, and its chaste, elegant details. Built in 1762–1768 by the architect Ange-Jacques Gabriel (1698–1782), this small château has been regarded as the most perfect example of French neoclassical architecture due to its form, which is simply based on a cube, and its discreet use of ornament in the Corinthian order.

The Petit Trianon was a favorite model for grand houses of the rich built across the United States in the period between 1890 and 1925. Influenced perhaps by the legend of Marie-Antoinette and partly by the calm beauty of the structure, American architects and patrons were drawn to the Petit Trianon as the height of conservative sophistication and good taste.[1] Starting with the most sumptuous of the Newport cottages, Marble House (fig. 1), built by Richard Morris Hunt (1827–1895) for the Vanderbilts in 1888–1892, the Petit Trianon gained ground as the ideal inspiration for a country house in the two following decades. Fueled by the enormous fortunes of the Gilded Age, variations sprang up across the United States.

In California, where country-house building was as active as on the East Coast around 1900, several versions were constructed. The first, the Petit Trianon in Cupertino built for wine producer Charles A. Baldwin in 1892, followed its model in name only. Completed the same year as Marble House, it was designed by Willis Polk (1867–1924) as a single-story pavilion with a porch of Ionic columns, a design that was closer to, if anything, the Grand Trianon. One of the earliest, more direct translations of the Petit Trianon, also in California, is a townhouse rather than a country house, built at 3800 Washington Street in the Pacific Heights neighborhood of San Francisco (fig. 2). Designed by the architect Frank van Trees for Marcus Koshland in 1902, it is built of a pinkish stone but follows the design of the original faithfully on its main facade. Also in California, San Jose's Petit Trianon Theater, built in 1923, is a broader translation for a larger, urban building with a different function. At the grand mansion constructed for railroad magnate Henry Huntington

Fig. 1 Marble House, Newport, Rhode Island, designed by Richard Morris Hunt for Mr. and Mrs. William K. Vanderbilt, 1888–1892. The design is based partly on the Petit Trianon but combines aspects of the Grand Trianon and even Versailles in the interiors.

Fig. 2 Koshland House, 3800 Washington Street, San Francisco, designed by Frank Van Trees for Marcus Koshland, 1902. A textbook translation of the Petit Trianon

in San Marino, California, the walls of the large drawing room are derived from the paneling of the *salon de compagnie* at the Petit Trianon (figs. 3, 4). Executed by the London decorating firm of White Allom around 1910 at the instigation of the art dealer Joseph Duveen, these elegant rooms were meant to house the early stages of the Huntington collections of art.[2]

Elsewhere in the United States the Petit Trianon served as a model for grand mansions. The distinguished firm of Carrère and Hastings designed the Nemours Mansion in Wilmington, Delaware, for Alfred Dupont in 1909. It follows the general design of the original but includes a somewhat incongruous hipped roof. The governor's mansion in Frankfort, Kentucky (fig. 5), designed by C. C. and E. A. Weber of Fort Mitchell and completed in 1914, doubles up the famous columns of the portico but otherwise adheres to the general design. There are further versions of the Petit Trianon in Chicago[3] and in Richmond, Virginia.[4] Even modern hotels have banquet rooms named for the Petit Trianon, but more for their association with a French royal château than for the architecture.[5] In this way the Petit Trianon has passed into the general culture of the United States, sometimes without any apparent connection to the original.

The popularity of the Petit Trianon as an architectural model in the United States seems to have been inspired by two very different

Fig. 3 The Large Drawing Room, Huntington Mansion, San Marino, California, designed by White Allom and Co., London, completed ca. 1910. The paneling and chimney-piece are based on the *salon de compagnie* of the Petit Trianon (see fig. 5). Courtesy of the Huntington Library, Art Collections, and Botanical Gardens, San Marino, California

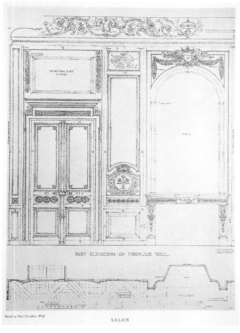

Fig. 4 Measured drawing of the *salon de compagnie* at the Petit Trianon. Plate 42 from James A. Arnott and John Wilson, *The Petit Trianon Versailles,* first published in 1907 (Reprint of 1929 by William Helburn, New York)

and apparently unconnected reasons. The training of American architects at the Ecole des Beaux-Arts in Paris is one obvious factor. Hunt was the first to have studied there, beginning in 1846. Henry Hobson Richardson (1838–1886) followed him, as did Charles F. McKim (1847–1909) of McKim, Mead and White, who designed the ultimate Beaux-Arts–inspired building, Pennsylvania Station (now demolished) in New York. This Paris school gave a solid academic training based on the supremacy of classicism and imbued the young American architects with the traditions of specifically French classicism. It was at the Ecole that American architects perhaps learned about the perfection of form, scale, and proportions of Gabriel's Petit Trianon. When Hunt designed Marble House, he took one of the teachings of the Beaux-Arts to heart by not slavishly copying any one structure but rather combining aspects of the Petit Trianon, the Grand Trianon, and even Versailles in one luxurious villa. Of course, it was no problem for his client, the socially ambitious Alva Vanderbilt (1853–1933), that the models were mostly royal palaces. Laurel Court in Cincinnati, designed by James Gamble Rogers (1867–1947) for Peter G. Thompson, founder of Champion Paper, was one of the grandest country houses of the era. Built between 1902 and 1907 it is, again, a synthesis of the Grand Trianon and the Petit Trianon rather than a direct copy of either one. Other American architects were less squeamish about using the Petit Trianon as a direct model, and thus the appearance of the more literal interpretations of the Petit Trianon in San Francisco, Delaware, and Kentucky mentioned above. The publication of the measured drawings of the Petit Trianon in England in 1907 and in the United States by the Boston Architectural Club in 1913 only fanned the flames (fig. 4).[6]

The second reason for the Petit Trianon's architectural legacy is the romantic legend of Marie-Antoinette. The story of the ill-fated queen of France had become almost a cult during the mid-nineteenth century, after the example of Empress Eugénie (1826–1920), the wife of Napoleon III. The empress had a fascination with the former queen of France, identifying perhaps with her own position as a foreign-born monarch. In emulation of Marie-Antoinette she was painted by Winterhalter in eighteenth-century dress (fig. 37). Her admiration for the queen even extended to her jewels, which were were designed in a consciously eighteenth-century style (cat. 20)—so much so that when the French crown jewels were sold by the Third Republic in 1887 some of the former empress's pieces were erroneously thought to have been Marie-Antoinette's.[7] The empress assembled furniture associated with the queen in her rooms at the Château de Saint-Cloud (fig. 38), and in the 1860s she instituted the restoration of the Petit Trianon. Under her aegis an exhibition on Marie-Antoinette was mounted there as part of the Paris Exposition of 1867. Visitors from around the world came to see the furniture and objects associated with the queen, culled from what was left of the former royal collections after the depredations of the French Revolution. Thus the Petit Trianon became focused not only on Marie-Antoinette; it was also the first museum to be devoted to objects of the Louis XVI style. Objects in the so-called Louis Seize taste and anything associated with Marie-Antoinette became the rage in the late nineteenth and early twentieth centuries, spreading to America during the Gilded Age.

Fig. 5 The Governor's Mansion, Frankfort, Kentucky, designed by C. C. and E. A. Weber of Fort Mitchell, completed in 1914. Courtesy of the Kentucky Division of Historic Properties

Although the heyday of buildings inspired by the Petit Trianon was over in the United States by 1930, this château and its gardens still held their appeal for Americans. The Petit Trianon became the beneficiary of American philanthropy in the twentieth century. John D. Rockefeller Jr. and his family funded the restoration of the gardens and the Hameau in the 1930s. The American-based World Monuments Fund contributed to the restoration of the Theater of the Petit Trianon in the 1990s, and the American Friends of Versailles have recently funded the restoration of the Pavillon Frais, a garden pavilion from the time of Louis XV. American fascination with Marie-Antoinette has persisted in the form of movies and books, which, when combined with a continuing admiration for the perfection of the architecture and the charm of the gardens of the Petit Trianon, has ensured that Americans are still drawn to this enchanting domain.

NOTES

With thanks to Fern Prosnitz for her assiduous research for this essay. —M.C.

1. Not only Americans—the French architect René Sergent built versions of the Petit Trianon in Paris in these years, such as the Duveen showroom behind the Place Vendôme and a house for the Camondo banking family in the Parc Monceau, now the musée Nissim de Camondo, completed in 1914.

2. Martin Chapman, "Richness and Refinement: The Taste for Gilt Bronzes in the Huntington Collection," *Catalogue of French Art* (New Haven: Yale University Press, forthcoming).

3. 1524 Lake Shore Drive by Howard Van Doren of 1917.

4. 909 West Franklin Street by Noland and Baskerville, 1911; although this version is more like Marble House in Newport than the Petit Trianon.

5. The Hilton Hotel in New York and the Beverly Wilshire in Beverly Hills, California.

6. James A. Arnott and John Wilson, *The Petit Trianon Versailles* (London, B. T. Batsford, 1907); *The Petit Trianon; Being a reproduction of plates from a work by James A. Arnott and John Wilson, Architects of Edinburgh,* Boston Architectural Club Year Book, 1913 (New York: New York Architectural Book Publishing Company, 1913).

7. Empress Eugénie's magnificent pearl tiara made by Lemonnier in 1853 was acquired by the princes of Thurn und Taxis at the 1887 sale because it was thought to have belonged to Marie-Antoinette. The jewel called the *broche reliquaire,* also made for the empress, was reserved from the sale because it was thought to be from the eighteenth century. Bernard Morel, *French Crown Jewels* (Antwerp: Fonds Mercator, 1988).

The History of the Petit Trianon

Pierre-Xavier Hans

The Trianon palace and garden, established by Louis XIV, would become a special place for his great-grandson Louis XV. In a part of the Trianon grounds devoted to nurseries for plants and trees, the latter king built a small private estate, beginning in 1749, to which he then added a "menagerie" of domesticated animals and a new garden. The royal architect Ange-Jacques Gabriel created a vegetable garden with a pavilion, as well as a barn, sheepfold, henhouse, and dairy (cat. 26).[1]

To mark the intersection of the two axes that defined the new King's Garden, Gabriel built a small pavilion intended for games, concerts, and refreshments: the French Pavilion (fig. 7), an exquisite structure that represents Louis XV's architectural ideal. It had an axial plan with an octagonal salon. In 1751 the king had the Pavillon Frais ("cool" pavilion) built to the southwest of the French Pavilion as a counterpart to the menagerie. Intended for use as a summer dining room, it was a rectangular pavilion with trelliswork covering its main facade.[2]

These developments further inspired Louis XV to add a small château to the Trianon estate, a special residence where he could stay with his mistress, Madame de Pompadour, and certain loyal followers. This new addition, the Petit Trianon (fig. 8), was already envisioned in 1758. Since the estate was primarily made up of gardens, the château would be open to the landscape on all sides.

The architect conceived the building to be appreciated from the gardens. The exterior decoration was in the Corinthian order, a return to antiquity owing to the influence of Madame de Pompadour, who, along with her brother, the Marquis de Marigny, director-general of the king's buildings, extolled the neoclassical aesthetic. The sculptor Honoré Guibert, an artist who was close to Marigny, created the sculptural program in the Greek style.

Construction of the Petit Trianon began in May 1762. The structure was erected in 1763–1764, and the interior work of sculpture, carpentry, painting, and ironwork was carried out in 1765–1768. By June 1769 Louis XV was dining in his new château, and he slept there

Fig. 6 Aerial view of the Petit Trianon and grounds

Fig. 7 The French Pavilion, designed for Louis XV by Ange-Jacques Gabriel, 1750

Fig. 8 The Petit Trianon, designed for Louis XV by Ange-Jacques Gabriel, 1762–1764

for the first time on September 9, 1770. He was immensely pleased with the new building. Gabriel had responded perfectly to the project he had been assigned: to create a pleasure house at the center of a garden, for use by the king and a privileged few. The building was on a human scale, devoid of pomp yet possessing an almost extravagant refinement. The luxury of the interior shone in every detail.

The Petit Trianon is composed of three levels: a ground floor, a second floor (*l'étage noble*) with a partial mezzanine, and an attic. The stair hall is the château's most spectacular space (fig. 9). To the west are two fruit cellars, originally intended to house the mechanism for two *tables volantes*. Louis XV had hoped to equip the dining room with mechanical tables that could be raised from the basement already laden with food, so that servants would not be needed. In the end, the state of the royal finances denied him this luxury; only the masonry footings in the cellar that were to hold the system of counterweights were built. Most of the rooms on the second floor were intended for receiving guests. On the staircase landing are two doors. One opens to an antechamber and a buffet room, at the southwest corner. This antechamber precedes a large dining room, which extends into a small dining room at the southeast corner. To the north, the *salon de compagnie* (salon or drawing room) is situated for protection from the summer heat. Along the east side were

Fig. 9 The stair hall of the Petit Trianon

Fig. 10 Detail of the wall paneling in the dining room, carved by Honoré Guibert about 1765

three rooms for the king's private use, with a mezzanine above them intended for the king's first valet. The other door on the landing leads to the attic floor, which housed the private apartment of Louis XV on the east, comprising three rooms followed by six so-called nobles' apartments.

Bringing the outside in is a recurring theme of the Petit Trianon. The staircase, with its sculpted ornamentation, carries elements of the exterior architecture into the heart of the château. The floor of the stair hall is tiled in veined white marble and green Campan marble. Green is a favored color in the château's decorative scheme, reflecting the greenery of the surrounding garden. The stone is complemented beautifully by the richly ornamented wrought-iron balustrade of the staircase, fashioned by François Brochois, in which Marie-Antoinette's monogram replaces that of Louis XV (fig. 41).

Inspired by its garden setting, the château's interior design incorporates fruits and flowers. The remarkable paneling in the dining room, carved by Guibert, is decorated with fruit garlands and baskets (fig. 10), and that in the salon with all kinds of flowers. The ornament of the paneling and the cornices above the doorways stands out in white against a sea green background. All of the over-door paintings illustrate subjects relating to flora. Charles-Nicolas Cochin, secretary of the Académie royale de peinture, announced the program to the king's painters in February 1768. "It is in this pleasure house that the king keeps his most beautiful flowers; I have sought subjects for the over-door paintings that would allow the inclusion of flowers, drawn from *Metamorphoses*."[3]

The decor and the furniture of the Petit Trianon also followed this naturalistic theme. The furniture, in the new Transitional style, reflecting the evolution from rococo to neoclassicism, was utterly sumptuous. Notwithstanding its country setting, the Petit Trianon required supremely rich furnishings for the king. The combination of the magnificent floral decorative scheme and the classical ornamentation created harmony between the Transitional-style furniture and the neoclassical interior design in the style that would be named for Louis XVI, with its clean lines.

The large dining room, which has three windows opening to the French Garden, received the most luxurious decor. The palette of the interior complemented that of the gardens, and the decor reflected the function of the space. The pale green background of the paneling, the carved ornament painted white, the crimson red of the *gros de Tours* curtains, and the brilliant gold of the frames of the mirrors and paintings produced a harmonious whole (fig. 44). Formerly lining the walls were twenty-four side chairs supplied by Claude-François Capin, His Majesty's official furnisher, with carved and painted wood decoration "in the antique style, following the taste of the apartment."[4] The first piece that the royal Garde-Meuble delivered was a higher chair for the king—even in his pleasure house, the king could not escape etiquette. At the center of the room hung a large gilt-bronze lantern, "a new model, in the antique style." All the rooms were provided with lanterns because they were subject to drafts.

The large salon, or drawing room, also featured a floral decor (fig. 11). The king's monogram was set in leaves through which grow three realistic lilies, surmounted by a crown of flowers (fig. 18). Capin supplied for Louis XV eighteen side chairs, a sofa, six armchairs, a folding screen, a firescreen, and a high chair. These chairs, made by the Foliot family, displayed richly carved wood painted white and damask upholstery with three colors on a crimson background.

The room beneath the mezzanine, the present *cabinet des glaces mouvantes* (Boudoir of Moving Mirrors), was a staircase. The middle

Fig. 11 The *salon de compagnie*

room was Louis XV's *cabinet de retraite* (retreat room) and later bed-room, with two windows opening to the botanical garden. For this room Guibert provided superb carved paneling adorned with real-istically portrayed daisies, suns, and buttercups. This room would become Madame Du Barry's bedchamber in 1772 and then Marie-Antoinette's in 1779, when the queen began to sleep at the Petit Trianon. On June 21, 1772, the furniture, made by the Foliots, was delivered to Madame Du Barry's room.[5]

The attic story offered the most beautiful views of the gardens. An antechamber opened to the king's apartment, which looked out toward the botanical garden. His bedroom contained magnificent gilt furniture, delivered by Capin, covered in superb "crimson and white lampas with Chinese figures."

When Marie-Antoinette made the Petit Trianon her private retreat, she retained the furnishings of the suite of reception rooms. Her use of the individual rooms on the second floor was different, however, and she ordered the demolition of the king's private stair-case to create a new boudoir. In 1776, she had the engineer Jean-Tobie Mercklein install mirrors that could be raised from beneath the floor to cover the north window, which opened directly onto the terrace (figs. 47–48).[6] At the same time, Foliot was ordered to restore the bed and chairs that furnished the former bedroom of Madame Du Barry, and Capin changed their fabric, covering the set in "pekin with nat-uralistic flowers and birds painted on white."[7] Capin delivered the painted furniture to the queen's bedroom on February 1, 1777.

In 1782 and 1783 the former nobles' apartments on the attic floor were joined to house Madame Royale, while Madame Elisabeth occu-pied the room of her brother, the king. Other changes instituted by Marie-Antoinette included moving the billiard table from the ground floor to the small dining room on the second floor. At this time she acquired increasingly sumptuous furniture, such as the fall-front sec-retary, in marquetry with mosaic sunflower designs in rich bronzes, delivered by Jean-Henri Riesener in 1783 (figs. 21–22).[8]

In 1786 the queen ordered the complete refurnishing of her châ-teau. She began, it appears, with two rooms reserved for her private use. Under the direction of the architect Richard Mique, the Rous-seau brothers created the wall decoration in the Boudoir of Moving Mirrors. Executed in the arabesque style, the panels featured white relief carving on a blue background in the fashion of Wedgwood cameos. The ornamental motifs include lyres, bouquets of roses, and scrolling arabesques of foliage (fig. 19).

The queen's Garde-Meuble ordered new furnishings for the bou-doir by the cabinetmaker Georges Jacob, probably based on designs by Jean-Démosthène Dugourc. The set comprised a daybed, three armchairs, and two side chairs, all upholstered in splendid blue peau de soie (fine grosgrain silk) "completely covered in white silk embroidery and lace." The embroidery and the pearl and silk fringes were mirrored in the curtains; the rich carving of the chairs was in the latest style.[9]

About 1785 Pierre-Philippe Thomire created for the queen a mon-umental lantern, which was also most likely designed by Dugourc (cat. 41). The spectacular object was installed in the salon, which otherwise retained its furniture from 1768.

The queen then remodeled her bedroom. In 1787 she ordered new furniture in a picturesque style that harmonized with the rural setting of the Petit Trianon (fig. 12). The design was surely by Dugourc. Basketwork patterns adorn the wood furniture, which was made by Georges Jacob.[10] In 1788 Thomire produced a set of gilt-bronze furnishings, including the clock and the wall lights, which take up the trelliswork motif. Jean-Ferdinand-Joseph Schwerdfeger delivered a mahogany chest of drawers, a console, and a *table en corbeille*. The so-called *chambre à coucher de treillage* (Trellis Bedroom) revealed the queen's taste for the rustic—falsely rustic because it was so sophisticated.

Fig. 12 Marie-Antoinette's bedroom

Taking the rustic aesthetic a step further, Marie-Antoinette had a picturesque English garden designed to replace Louis XV's botanical garden. As of July 10, 1774, the comte de Caraman submitted his design for a new garden. Richard Mique, Hubert Robert, the gardener Antoine Richard, and the comte de Caraman worked together on the execution of this garden between 1774 and 1783.[11] The guiding principle was to combine masses of greenery, hillocks, boulders, and water features to create a "natural" landscape, which is arranged to emphasize vistas into the distance.[12] These vistas were punctuated with picturesque follies, small ornamental pavilions in romantic, classical, or exotic (even Chinese) styles.

To the north of the Petit Trianon arose the Belvedere Rock, culminating in the Belvedere itself, a neoclassical structure in complete contrast with the Rock, which offered a magnificent panorama of the Trianon garden. Another landscape feature was the Montagne de l'Escargot, a miniature world with spiraling paths that concealed Marie-Antoinette's famous yet mysterious grotto, built with blocks of millstone (cat. 63D). The slopes were planted with mountain trees and vines. The wide variety of tree species at the

Trianon is a testament to the botanical exchanges between Europe and North America during that period. To the east, a river leads to the Temple of Love, a rotunda with twelve Corinthian columns, which is set on a large island. At the northwest corner the Chinese *jeu de bague* (merry-go-round) and a Chinese gallery evoke an oriental fantasy (cat. 63A). The garden at the Petit Trianon was specially conceived for nighttime festivities, in which the architecture and the lake would be illuminated (cat. 64).

The rustic aesthetic seen in the English garden of the Petit Trianon culminates in the Hameau, a hamlet that Mique built for Marie-Antoinette beginning in 1783, based on an idea by Hubert Robert. The Hameau comprised eleven thatched cottages in a rustic Normandy style and of Flemish inspiration, arranged around a vast artificial pond. Amid this contrived setting, where she strolled with her children and entertained her guests, Marie-Antoinette nonetheless established a small working farm.

The queen's idyllic life at the Petit Trianon came to an end with her imprisonment and eventual execution. The sale beginning in August 1793 dispersed the furniture from the estate, and for a time the château served as cafe and pleasure garden. When the emperor Napoleon made his first visit to the estate on March 13, 1805, he decided to reclaim the building that had been abandoned to popular use. The refurnished Petit Trianon was put at the disposal of his sister Pauline, Princess Borghese, and she moved there in June 1805. After 1809 Napoleon ordered new furniture for his palaces, and the two Trianons were again refurnished. He offered the Petit Trianon to the new empress, Marie-Louise, to whom the furniture left by Pauline Borghese appeared relatively simple; its luxury was not sufficient for an empress.

The empress's bedroom, formerly that of Marie-Antoinette, was given a tent-shaped decor and an antique-style bed adorned with winged figures. Sky-blue satin concealed the paneling, while the ceiling was in white satin trimmed with blue silk and gold. Clearly the room was sumptuous, and the artifice of the tent succeeded in obliterating the simplicity of the space. The decorator François-Louis-Castelnaux Darrac delivered the satin furnishings; Pierre-Benoît Marcion executed the gilt-wood furniture.[13]

In the next generation, Louis-Philippe allotted the Petit Trianon to his eldest son, Ferdinand, duc d'Orléans. These two were the last princes to live there. The château was completely renovated for the heir to the throne and the princess, who took possession of the estate on October 5, 1837. The apartments mixed the Empire furniture with new pieces, and the textile decor was replaced to suit contemporary tastes. The chairs dating to the Empire were recovered in printed Persian cloth.

After the fall of Louis-Philippe, the Petit Trianon, though uninhabited, retained this furniture until 1867. Then Empress Eugénie, moved by a real passion for the unfortunate queen, decided to turn the château into a museum dedicated to Marie-Antoinette. On the occasion of the Paris Exposition of 1867, she sought to reconstitute the state of the Petit Trianon as Marie-Antoinette had known it.[14] There she assembled some remarkable Louis XVI furnishings, a great many of the pieces and art objects having belonged to the queen. Most of this furniture is still in place today, on public view.

On May 21, 1867, the empress opened the Petit Trianon to the public, ostensibly furnished as in Marie-Antoinette's day. On the staircase visitors could admire the lantern by Thomire, which Napoleon I had repurchased. But it was the queen's former billiard room that held the exhibition's masterpiece: Marie-Antoinette's jewel cabinet, a sumptuous piece ordered by the queen in 1787 and executed by Schwerdfeger, probably based on Dugourc's designs (fig. 15). In the salon stood the elaborate mechanical table executed by Riesener and ordered by Pierre-Elisabeth de Fontanieu for his use in Paris in 1771. The "table of the Muses" was an already famous piece that was thought to have belonged to Marie-Antoinette.

In the former Boudoir of Moving Mirrors was the magnificent writing table in Japanese lacquer by Adam Weisweiler, supplied by the merchant Dominique Daguerre in 1784 for Marie-Antoinette's *cabinet doré* in Versailles. Also on display was the console carved by the Rousseau brothers for the *boudoir de la méridienne* at Versailles in 1781, on loan from Baron Double (fig. 29). In the dressing room, one could admire Marie-Antoinette's dressing table from the Tuileries, delivered in 1784; it would remain at the Trianon (cat. 58). The exhibition was a great success. Afterward the works on loan from collectors were returned, but many of those obtained from the Garde-Meuble would remain at Versailles. From that point on, the memory of Marie-Antoinette would be definitively associated with the Trianon. Advances in knowledge and in acquisition and conservation policies have accelerated the refurnishing of the château. Nonetheless, the loss of the archives of the queen's private Garde-Meuble prevents us from gaining a precise view of the Petit Trianon's interior furnishings.[15]

The splendid lantern by Thomire that Marie-Antoinette ordered has reclaimed its place in the salon. In substitution for the Foliot chairs, a set of handsome Louis XVI chairs by Jean-Baptiste Sené, covered in three-colored lampas, has occupied the room since 1973; it came to the Petit Trianon in 1868 (cat. 45). Flanking the fireplace is a pair of *bergères* by the Foliots that had been brought to Château de Saint-Hubert in 1771 for the comtesse Du Barry; they were acquired in 1994, along with the matching firescreen (cat. 44). They offer the best illustration of the Trianon's original Transitional furniture, delivered to Louis XV. The gaming table in wild cherry, delivered by Gilles Joubert in 1768 and acquired by Versailles in 1985, is the sole example of the furniture made for Louis XV (cat. 25). The museum has acquired the suite of chairs from the so-called *meuble des épis* ("wheat-ear" furniture) executed by Jacob for Marie-Antoinette's bedroom, namely, two armchairs, two side chairs, a firescreen, and a footstool (cat. 55). The original bed, however, could not be found and has been reproduced. The cotton fabric is printed with a simplified design imitating the original embroidered fabric. The large mahogany console executed by Schwerdfeger, with its extraordinary gilt-bronze decoration, was acquired in 1976 (cat. 56). Thus, the Trellis Bedroom has almost all its furniture back (fig. 12).

At the Trianon, the perfection of the architecture and interior design inspired perfection in the furnishings. The Transitional pieces provided to Louis XV were particularly compatible with the paneled decor. After the Revolution the château contained the Empire furniture intended for Pauline Borghese and then the more luxurious pieces delivered to the empress Marie-Louise. But the furnishings created for Marie-Antoinette, with their tasteful and elegant floral decoration, were truly in accord with the château's Louis XVI–style architecture. This harmony can still be appreciated today, for the refurnished Petit Trianon remains fresh and alive.

NOTES

1. Christian Baulez, "Le nouveau Trianon," in *Les Gabriel,* ed. Michel Gallet and Yves Bottineau (Paris: Picard, 1982), 168.

2. Demolished in 1810, it was rebuilt in 1980 but without its interior decor or its garden.

3. Baulez, *Visite du Petit Trianon et du Hameau de la Reine* (Versailles: Art Lys, 1996), 15.

4. Baulez, "Le Domaine de Trianon," *Connaissance de Paris et de la France,* no. 35 (1977): 21.

5. Ibid., 24.

6. Baulez, *Visite,* 28.

7. Baulez, "Domaine," 25.

8. It is now in the Wallace Collection, London.

9. Baulez, "Domaine," 26.

10. The *bergère* has not been located; the dressing chair is in the collection of the J. Paul Getty Museum in Los Angeles.

11. Pierre-André Lablaude, *Les Jardins de Versailles* (Paris: Scala, 1995), 137–161.

12. Laurent Choffé, "Le Jardin Champêtre de Trianon," *Versalia: revue de la Société des Amis de Versailles,* no. 7 (2007): 58.

13. Denise Ledoux-Lebard, *Versailles: Le Petit Trianon, le mobilier des inventaires de 1807, 1810 et 1839* (Paris: Editions de l'Amateur, 1989), 102.

14. Baulez, "Le remeublement de Versailles," in *De Versailles à Paris: le destin des collections royales,* ed. Jacques Charles (Paris: Centre culturel du Panthéon, 1989), 204.

15. Daniel Meyer, "Les antichambres et les salons du Petit Trianon," *Revue du Louvre,* no. 3 (1976): 208–212.

VENTE

DE
MEUBLES ET EFFETS
DE LA CI - DEVANT REINE,
PROVENANT DU PETIT TRIANON,
EN VERTU DE LA LOI DU DIX JUIN DERNIER,

Le Dimanche 25 Août 1793, l'an deuxième de la République une & indivisible, 10 heures du matin, & 4 heures de relevée, & jours suivans.

SAVOIR:

Tous les matins. Batterie & uftenfiles de cuifine & d'office, ferraillés & meubles communs. *Tous les foirs.* Meubles de fuite, confiftans en Lits avec leurs houffes de différentes étoffes, armoires, fecrétaires, commodes, tables, confoles, partie à deffus de marbre; feux, chaifes longues, fauteuils, canapés, banquettes, chaifes à tabourets de damas, lampas, velours de foie d'Utrecht, & moquette; faïence, verrerie, porcelaine d'office & de table.

Les autres Meubles de toute efpèce, & en grande quantité, feront annoncés par de nouvelles affiches.

Cette vente fe fera en préfence des Repréfentans du Peuple, & des Commiffaires du Diftrict, au ci-devant Château de Verfailles.

N. B. Les Meubles de la ci-devant Lifte civile peuvent être tranfportés à l'étranger, en exemption de tous droits.

Les Commiffaires de la Convention Nationale.
CH. DELACROIX, J. M. MUSSET.

DE L'IMPRIMERIE NATIONALE.

Preciousness, Elegance, and Femininity: The Personal Taste of Queen Marie-Antoinette

Martin Chapman

Marie-Antoinette's taste has been viewed through different lenses over the centuries, colored very much according to the viewer's political persuasion. Thomas Jefferson, while American ambassador to France in 1787, had little good to say about the queen, complaining that she was "devoted to pleasure and expense."[1] His successor, Gouverneur Morris, who admired the queen's furniture to the extent of acquiring some choice pieces during the Revolution,[2] nevertheless lamented the expense of the queen's gardens of the Petit Trianon when he visited during the fateful summer of 1789.[3] This reputation for frivolity and extravagance obliterated any appreciation for the beauty of the queen's furnishings and decorations during the Revolution. The contents of the Petit Trianon were sold beginning in August 1793 as if ridding the state of any connections with Marie-Antoinette (see poster of the Petit Trianon sale, fig. 13).

When the pendulum swung back during the second half of the nineteenth century, and Marie-Antoinette's reputation was cast as a tragic heroine rather than a spendthrift, a thriving market was created in objects associated with the queen. The Rothschilds collected her pieces fervently. By 1900 it seemed that almost any object perceived as French and of late eighteenth-century origin could have been Marie Antoinette's, resulting in many false attributions and a virtual industry in pieces, particularly porcelain, made in the presumed style of the queen. After scientific studies in the 1930s allowed the stamps on royal furniture to be decoded, and the archives of the former royal household were studied systematically, a more accurate understanding of the queen's taste began to emerge.[4] Opinions since then have been polarized: one camp still sees her taste as vapid, costly, and showy, while the other views it as more precious and sophisticated, citing the beautiful objects and decorations made for her. Because so little documentary evidence survives about the queen's own opinions in matters of taste it is still difficult to say exactly what she commissioned according to her personal inclinations and what was purveyed to her by the royal architects, designers, and *intendants* (supervisors of the queen's furnishings).[5]

Fig. 13 Poster advertising the sale of the contents of the Petit Trianon, August 25, 1793. By kind permission of the trustees of The Wallace Collection, London

This rare poster shows that the sale of the "furniture and effects of the former queen" was put into law on June 10. The contents were sold beginning August 25, 1793, with the furniture auctioned in the evening sessions. The note at the bottom indicates that the furniture could be exported tax free, which would have been useful to collectors like James Swan of Boston, who acquired several pieces from the queen's bedroom suite and the pair of firedogs from the Hameau (cat. 75).

Fig. 14 Gabriel Jacques de Saint-Aubin (1724–1780), *Goût de la Reine pour les Arts* (The Queen's Taste for the Arts), 1775. Drawing from *Placets de l'officier Desbans* (Petitions by the Officer Desbans to Queen Marie-Antoinette and King Louis XVI). Private collection

This drawing shows the shows the queen as a protector of the Arts, with a painting on the easel beside her and prints on the ground in front of her. One Cupid offers the queen a brush, another an engraving tool.

Fig. 15 Jean-Ferdinand-Joseph Schwerdfeger (1734–1818), Marie-Antoinette's jewel cabinet, 1787. Musée du Château de Versailles

The central panel by Louis-Simon Boizot depicts the Arts.

This essay can neither answer this question definitively nor take on the polarized opinions that go back some two hundred years, but in addressing some of the schemes of decoration and furnishings made for the queen, particularly those of the Petit Trianon, it can bring us closer to what surely must have been Marie-Antoinette's personal taste.

Marie-Antoinette was expected to be a patron of taste; such was one of the many roles allotted to her as a queen. Therefore, she was obliged to commission the finest examples of French design and craftsmanship available. As with her dress, which was required to be of the latest Parisian fashion, yet of a type appropriate for a queen,[6] the design and decoration of her apartments reflected who the queen was meant to be as much as her own personal taste. An early example of this role is suggested by a 1775 drawing (fig. 14) by Gabriel de Saint Aubin (1724–1780) depicting the "Goût de la Reine pour les Arts" (Queen's Taste for the Arts) as one of her attributes.[7] Even though this drawing was made when Marie-Antoinette was only twenty years old, it demonstrated the notion that the queen of France was to be the protector or patron of the Arts. As late as 1787, when Jefferson was complaining about her extravagance, this idea was still being promoted. On her great jewel cabinet, supplied that year, there is a central plaque that depicts the Arts (fig. 15). The plaque's prominent position on the cabinet proclaims its subject as the main attribute of the queen. Indeed, the queen did patronize painters and sculptors, notably Madame Elisabeth Vigée Le Brun (1755–1842) as her portraitist (cats. 15, 16) and Louis-Simon Boizot (1743–1809) as her sculptor (cats. 6, 7, 29, 30). However, her interest in painting was restricted to portraiture and genre scenes and did not encompass the grand tradition of history painting.[8] Madame Campan, the queen's lady-in-waiting, famously remarked on the queen's preferences in painting and the poor quality of the artists who worked for the queen

Fig. 16 The queen's bedchamber at Versailles. The textile hangings are modern reweavings of those by Defarges of Lyon, installed in 1786.

in the early years of her reign.[9] But while the young queen's choice of painters may be deemed inferior—though some would argue that her choice later of Vigée Le Brun did the queen a great service[10]—her patronage in the field of decoration, design, and furnishings reveals the more enduring aspects of her taste.

Although much redecoration and refurnishing of the royal palaces was executed during the reign of Louis XVI and Marie-Antoinette, certain factors could override the queen's authority and her taste. She was not able to freely dictate the design and decoration of the large formal rooms at Versailles because court tradition imposed certain rules. A well-known instance was when the queen appropriated the *salon de la paix* (Peace Salon) at the end of the *galerie des glaces* (Hall of Mirrors) as her gaming room. She was provided with some new furnishings in the latest neoclassical style, but she was not allowed to compromise the grandiose, baroque architectural identity of the room, so important was it judged that the style and structure of the Sun King's palace remain.[11] In the queen's formal bedchamber, now restored to what it must have looked like in Marie-Antoinette's time (fig. 16), the elaborate ceiling decoration was retained from the time of Marie-Thérèse, queen of Louis XIV, in the late seventeenth century. Only the magnificent bed and silk hangings were newly commissioned for Marie-Antoinette's occupation in 1770. An instance of the rapidly, almost quixotic, changes in the queen's taste occurred in conjunction with these hangings. The summer hangings of *gros de Tours*[12] supplied for her initial occupation were replaced in 1785 with a new blue and white set made by Pernon in Lyon. But, as the queen did not like these replacements, in the following year she commissioned a further set of hangings from Defarges, also of Lyon, costing the huge sum of 315 *livres* (pounds) an *aune*.[13] The refused set was sent to another palace, but the large expense of these changes only furthered the queen's reputation for extravagance. The hangings shown in the bedchamber today are a modern reweaving of this last set. The elaborate and rich pattern—featuring bouquets of flowers suspended from ribbons and peacock feathers, which are mythological emblems of Juno (queen of the gods)—indicates that the formality of the design reflected the queen's public image invented by her designers rather than her own taste.

If the public rooms at Versailles and other royal châteaux were subject to long-held rules and "official taste," Marie-Antoinette's *petits appartements* (private rooms) at Versailles and Fontainebleau, and the whole of the Petit Trianon, were areas where ostensibly her personal choices could prevail. In general terms the style employed in her private rooms was the elegant, luxurious, and yet restrained phase of neoclassicism prevalent the 1780s, sometimes known as *goût étrusque* (Etruscan taste) or *à l'antique* (antique taste). The interior decorative schemes of these rooms and their furnishings give a cogent view of the queen's aesthetic. It is difficult to see their delicate, yet rich, decoration, their remarkable sense of scale and proportion, their sumptuous upholstery, their exquisite craftsmanship, and their gilded details as anything other than a dazzling display of preciousness, elegance, and femininity.

These decorations and furnishings were executed for the queen by a team of architects, designers, decorators, carvers, cabinetmakers, upholsterers, silk manufacturers, and other specialized craftsmen in the luxury trades all working under the direction of the *intendant et contrôleur général des Meubles de la Couronne* (Superintendent of the Royal Furnishings).[14] As the *intendants* were in charge of the furnishing of the royal palaces, they became effectively the impresarios of royal taste. During the reign of Louis XVI and Marie-Antoinette, the first of these pivotal figures, Pierre-Elisabeth de Fontanieu (1731–1784), was a highly refined aristocrat and courtier. He directed the design and decoration of the royal apartments by exercising close control over the craftsmen working for the queen. He furthered the rise of Jean-Henri Riesener (1734–1806), the most important cabinetmaker in the years before the Revolution, who supplied many pieces for the queen (see cats. 42, 43; figs. 21–22). Fontanieu's interest in design extended to publishing his own series of prints of vases, *Collection de vases, inventés et dessinés par M. de Fontanieu* in 1770, some of which were later made in porcelain by the royal factory at Sèvres.[15] He was succeeded in 1784 by Marc-Antoine Thierry de la Ville d'Avray (1732–1792), also an aristocrat and courtier, who reorganized the ancient institution of the Garde-Meuble in an attempt to save money, but who in fact fomented a frenzy of decorating activity in the royal palaces. It could be argued reasonably that these men, who ensured the high quality of design and execution for the furnishing of the queen's apartments (and indeed all the royal palaces), were the true givers of taste to Marie-Antoinette.

The professional figures involved in the design and execution of work for the queen could also claim to be instigators of the queen's taste—and indeed did so. Under Fontanieu the designer Jacques Gondoin (1737–1818) supplied much work for the redecoration of the queen's private apartments and for the royal châteaux in general. He designed the first set of hangings of the queen's bedchamber mentioned above, and the decorations and furniture in her *cabinet intérieur* (private study) at Versailles, executed in 1779. The sofa from

Fig. 17 The *cabinet doré*, Marie-Antoinette's private study or boudoir at Versailles, was refurbished in 1783.

the suite supplied for this project (cat. 10) shows his rich interpretation of the neoclassical style, with its skilled carving of masses of tiny flower heads running along the frame and its scrolled arms emerging from horns of plenty. The latter motifs were mythological allusions to love and fecundity, subjects close to the queen's heart (see "Motherhood," p. 62). Gondoin's rich decorative scheme, which included lavish silk wall panels and upholstery with scrolling arabesques on a white silk ground (cat. 11), was swept away only a few years later in 1783–1784 by a more fashionable scheme. The result was the jewellike *cabinet doré* (gilded study) that survives today (fig. 17). The white and gold paneling, decorated with perfume burners, trophies, and sphinxes in the *goût étrusque*, epitomizes the delicacy, perfect proportion, and preciousness that have become associated with the queen's taste.

Jean-Démosthène Dugourc (1749–1825) took over control as *dessinateur* of the Garde-Meuble de la Couronne in 1784. He maintained in his autobiography of 1800 that he was the real impetus behind the design of the furniture and decoration made for the queen. Dugourc also claimed to be the pioneer of the *goût étrusque* and the leading arbiter of design in the decade before the Revolution.[16] He made designs for many of the queen's projects, such as a jewel cabinet[17] and the refurnishing of the Petit Trianon in the late 1780s.[18]

After Louis XVI gave Marie-Antoinette the Petit Trianon as her private estate in 1774, she instituted first a program of landscaping and then a campaign of furnishing that reflect her personal preferences most accurately. The landscaping in the form of a fashionable *jardin anglais* (English-style garden) was influenced by English gardens such as those built at Kew outside London in the 1750s, with their meandering landscape sprinkled decorously with pavilions, ruins, and a Chinese pagoda. For her project, the queen drew on a group of advisers under the hand of her architect Richard Mique. Although there were already precedents in France, the gardener Antoine Richard was not up to creating this new style of garden, and the comte de Caraman, who had his own *jardin anglais* at Roissy and had been to England, therefore advised. A hectic program of building—impatience seems to have been one of the queen's less fortunate traits—ensued from 1776 to 1782 (cat. 63). The planning of the landscape was changed on more than one occasion. The buildings, temples, and follies were designed in a wide range of styles. The Chinese-style merry-go-round of 1776 was followed by the classical Temple of Love in 1778. The Italianate Belvedere of 1778–1781 was built alongside the "natural" Rock, Cascade, and Grotto of 1779–1782 as a picturesque grouping. The queen's haste is documented in the furnishing of the Belvedere pavilion, which she insisted on being completed as quickly as possible (cat. 65).[19]

The ultimate folly was the next program of construction, the Hameau (Hamlet), the model village for which the gardens are most famous, built in 1783–1785 and later. This too was by no means the first such instance. The prince de Condé had built his hamlet at Chantilly a few years before, and the royal architect Mique must have been severely stretched by building yet another hamlet for the royal aunts at the château de Bellevue at the same time. The comtesse de Provence had her hamlet at Montreuil, and the comte d'Artois had a rustic garden at Raincy. In fact, there was an element of imitation and rivalry in these pleasure gardens, which must partly account for the reputation for frivolity held by all members of the royal family, and prominent members of the aristocracy, not just the queen. The Hameau at the Petit Trianon was perhaps the most successful iteration of all, with its picturesque group of Normandy-style thatched cottages, mill, and farmhouses artfully arranged around a lake in a composition designed by the painter Hubert Robert. There was even a working dairy and farm with a real farmer and his wife, as well as cows, ducks, and sheep. Although Marie-Antoinette may have turned her hand to making butter and cheese to experience the charms of rustic life, contrary to the well-worn myth she did not stagger under the weight of milk pails dressed as a dairymaid or get up in the guise as a shepherdess there—that was reserved for the amateur dramatics on the stage of her little theater nearby. The houses used by the queen at the Hameau were luxuriously furnished in the latest style of the mid-1780s, with plainer, English-style mahogany furniture for the dining room (cats. 72–74) that contrasted with sumptuous and meticulously made furnishings like the pair of gilt-bronze firedogs modeled as goats eating grapes, a reference to the classical rite of Bacchus (cat. 75). Somehow exquisitely crafted objects and decorations were always present alongside the rustic at the queen's Trianon.

In addition to the Garde-Meuble de la Couronne mentioned above, the queen had her own Garde-Meuble de la Reine, which supplied pieces for her as well. Under the direction of Bonnefoy du Plan, the

Fig. 18 Detail of paneling in the *salon de compagnie* of the Petit Trianon, carved by Honoré Guibert about 1765. Interlaced *L*s for Louis XV are entwined with lilies, flanked by sprays of laurel, and surmounted by a wreath of roses. There are also flower heads in the interlaced ornament below.

Fig. 19 Detail of the paneling in the *cabinet des glaces mouvantes* carved by the Rousseau brothers in 1787

Garde-Meuble de la Reine produced a wide range of furniture and decorations, including much that was supplied for the Petit Trianon in the late 1780s. Unfortunately its archives are lost.[20]

One area that we can say definitively was Marie-Antoinette's personal taste was her love of flowers, especially roses. Her public and private apartments reflected this passion, as did her furniture and her dress. An example of the queen's preferences is demonstrated by a dinner service, the *Service riche en couleurs et riche en or* (dinner service rich in color and rich in gold) that was made for her by the royal Sèvres factory in 1784 (cat. 13).[21] It is recorded that she chose the motifs, the strings of pearls and the flowers—roses, pansies, and cornflowers (bachelor's buttons)—that she favored at the Petit Trianon. Although flowers had been a decorative motif at the Petit Trianon since before the queen's time (they had been included in the decoration of the château from the outset, reflecting its role as a country house in a garden [see fig. 18 for a detail of the floral paneling in the salon from the 1760s]), flowers would feature prominently in the furnishings supplied for Marie-Antoinette at the Petit Trianon.

The queen's changes to the interiors at the Petit Trianon had been initially relatively minor in comparison with the work done elsewhere. It is thought that she did not want or need to change the decoration as recently installed as the late 1760s. The room she chose as her boudoir, next to her bedroom, known as the *cabinet des glaces mouvantes* (Boudoir of Moving Mirrors), was named for the mirrored shutters that rise out of the floor to cover the windows at night. These mirrors, engineered by Jean-Tobie Merklein, were intended to give both security and privacy to this most private of the queen's rooms, which opened directly onto a terrace. They rose from chambers built for them in the basement.

In 1786 Marie-Antoinette ordered the refurnishing the Petit Trianon. In addition, the Boudoir of Moving Mirrors was repaneled with detailed ornament of trophies, vases, and musical instruments suspended on ribbons, executed by the sculptors the Rousseau brothers and painted white on a pale blue ground resembling Wedgwood (fig. 19). This project, the only room at the Petit Trianon to be repaneled for the queen, was carried out under the direction of Bonnefoy du Plan in 1787. It is the essence of the style supplied for Marie-Antoinette; restrained in form, yet rich in detail, and executed with consummate craftsmanship.

Also in 1787 a new suite of furniture and furnishings for the queen's bedroom was undertaken by her Garde-Meuble. Probably made to the design of Dugourc, it is one of the most original suites of furniture ever conceived. Reflecting the charms of rustic life, flowers feature prominently, as well as trellis- and basketwork, and the decorative motifs are executed in minutely carved detail. Basketwork recurs in different materials: in wood on the carved seat rails of the chairs and in gilt bronze on the mounts of the mahogany furniture. The trelliswork from which the *chambre à coucher de treillage* (Trellis Bedroom) takes its name is incorporated into gilt-bronze furnishings made especially for the room by Pierre-Philippe Thomire (1751–1843), including a clock (cat. 57) and a pair of wall lights (fig. 20). Contrary to the usual surface treatment for royal furniture, the chairs are devoid of gilding, an intentional nod to their country-house setting. Instead, the decoration is painted in naturalistic colors to underscore the rustic quality. The uprights of the seats appear to be made out of reeds or sticks (or possibly even straw) bound together with garlands of ivy, ribbons, and jasmine. The chairs are further decorated with lilies of the valley, pinecone finials, and the wheat ears from which the suite takes its name, the *meuble des épis* ("wheat-ear" furniture) (cat. 55). On the mahogany console table made by Schwerdfeger, in

Fig. 20 Pierre-Philippe Thomire (1751–1843), pair of patinated and gilt bronze wall lights made for the *chambre à coucher de treillage* (Trellis Bedroom) at the Petit Trianon, 1787–1788. Museu Calouste Gulbenkian, Lisbon

These wall lights take up the trellis theme in the arms and the sockets for the candles. The central backplate is entwined with flowers.

Figs. 21–22 Jean-Henri Riesener (1734–1806), *secrétaire* (writing desk) supplied for the queen's use at the Petit Trianon on March 8, 1783. By kind permission of the trustees of The Wallace Collection, London

addition to the gilt-bronze basketwork mounts, there is a frieze of sunflowers and thistle leaves. Like the other ornamental details in this suite of furniture, the charming dogs' heads, which may represent the queen's pet dogs, are meticulously and naturalistically modeled (cat. 56).

Largely absent today from the Petit Trianon are the lavish pieces of furniture made for the queen by Jean-Henri Riesener, the queen's favorite cabinetmaker. Although he was supplanted as *ébéniste du roi* (king's cabinetmaker) in 1784 by Thierry de la Ville D'Avray's reforms to the Garde-Meuble, he still continued to supply pieces for the queen's use. She is known to have favored Riesener's rich style of cabinetmaking, in which marquetry or veneered-wood surfaces contrast with elaborate, almost jewel-like gilt-bronze mounts. For the Petit Trianon, which was deemed a private country house, the furniture was not intended to be as grand as the pieces made for the other, more public, royal palaces. The simple mahogany furniture Riesener made for the Hameau reflects this idea (cats. 72–74), yet some of the pieces he supplied for the queen's château are of a level of richness and sophistication on par with pieces made for other royal palaces. Supplied for the Petit Trianon in 1783, the *secrétaire* (writing desk), now in the Wallace Collection, shows the taste of and for the queen (figs. 21–22). Its scale is small, arguably to suit the proportion of the rooms, but otherwise its decoration is as rich, and possibly even richer, than other royal pieces made by Riesener, especially in its elaborate gilt-bronze mounts.[22] The marquetry panels, crisscrossed with trelliswork and decorated with sunflowers, are framed with gilt-bronze mounts crafted with dense ornament that is nothing short of astonishing in detail. Flowers are featured again; the roses, carnations entwined with ribbons, and wheat ears are similar to the motifs found on the *meuble des épis*. They are used in the complex interlaced frieze, while more garlands of these flowers, finished to the smallest detail, are draped and hung from the mounts on the corners.

These last pieces made for the Petit Trianon probably reflect most closely Marie-Antoinette's personal style in the late 1780s. Beautifully crafted, with a wealth of the floral details she favored, surely these projects were made to complement the queen's taste? Through their elegant, restrained designs and consummate craftsmanship, the objects and furnishings made by Marie-Antoinette's designers, architects, and *intendants* for her private use are superlative examples of eighteenth-century decorative arts, and in this endeavor the queen must have played an active part.

NOTES

1. *The Jeffersonian Cyclopedia* (New York and London: Funk and Wagnalls Co., 1900), letter no. 5051, p. 536.

2. For example, he acquired some of the seat furniture from the queen's *cabinet interieur* at Versailles (see cat. 10).

3. "Royalty has here endeavored at great expense to conceal itself from its own eye. But the attempt is vain. A dairy furnished with porcelain of Sèvres [it was in fact from the Paris rue Thiroux porcelain factory] is a semblance too splendid for rural life. . . . On the whole this garden is handsome and yet the money applied in making it has been but badly spent." Gouverneur Morris, *The Diary and Letters of Gouverneur Morris* (New York: Charles Scribner's Sons, 1888), vol.1, p. 82.

4. For example, in Pierre Verlet's *French Royal Furniture,* first published in 1963.

5. Eleanor Tollfree, "Le mobilier de Marie-Antoinette à la Wallace Collection," *Versalia,* no. 9 (2006): pp. 156–177.

6. Caroline Weber, *Queen of Fashion: What Marie Antoinette Wore to the Revolution* (New York: Henry Holt, 2006).

7. Everett Fahy, ed., *Wrightsman Pictures* (New York: Metropolitan Museum of Art, 2005), pp. 206, 208.

8. Colin B. Bailey, *Patriotic Taste: Collecting Modern Art in Pre-Revolutionary Paris* (New Haven and London: Yale University Press, 2002), pp. 167–168.

9. Boysson, Bernadette de, and Xavier Salmon, *Marie-Antoinette à Versailles: Le goût d'une reine* (Paris: Somogy éditions d'art, 2005), p. 78.

10. Joseph Baillio, *Elisabeth Vigée Le Brun* (Fort Worth: Kimbell Art Museum, 1982).

11. Christian Baulez, "Le grand cabinet intérieur de Marie Antoinette, Décor, mobilier et collections," in Monika Kopplin and Christian Baulez, *Les Laques de Japon, collections de Marie-Antoinette* (Paris: Réunion des musées nationaux, 2001), p. 29.

12. A heavy silk with a dull finish.

13. An *aune* (ell) was about 1.2 meters. Boysson and Salmon, pp. 120–121.

14. Also cited as *intendant du Garde-Meuble,* or *intendant général du Garde-Meuble,* and *Intendant et Contrôleur Général des Meubles de la Couronne.*

15. Svend Eriksen, *Early Neoclassicism in France* (London: Faber and Faber, 1974), pp. 180–181, 396, pls. 449–452.

16. Simon Jervis, *Dictionary of Design and Designers* (London: Penguin, 1984), p. 161.

17. Not extant, but a model for it dating from 1787 is in the Walters Art Museum, Baltimore.

18. Pierre Arizzoli-Clémentel, *Versailles: Furniture of the Royal Palace, 17th and 18th Centuries,* vol. 2 (Dijon: Editions Faton, 2002), p. 15.

19. Daniel Meyer, *Versailles: Furniture of the Royal Palace, 17th and 18th Centuries,* vol. 1 (Dijon: Editions Faton, 2002), p. 230.

20. Ibid., p. 260.

21. Boysson and Salmon, pp. 154–155.

22. Tollfree, "Le Mobilier de Marie-Antoinette à la Wallace Collection," pp. 156–178.

I The Life of Marie-Antoinette: Myth and Reality

More than two hundred years after her death, Marie-Antoinette (1755–1793) continues to fascinate a wide public. Her transition from the carefree, young queen to the woman who faced a terrible death during the French Revolution has inspired a host of myths, many of which have become embedded in our culture. On one side she is painted as a heroine and a saint martyred to the French Revolution; on the other side she is portrayed as a frivolous and extravagant airhead who spied for Austria, or, even worse, as a libertine and a whore. The reality is none of these personas. Stefan Zweig, one of her most perceptive biographers, describes her as an average woman in extraordinary circumstances.

"Let them eat cake," the famous phrase attributed to Marie-Antoinette about feeding the poor during the famine of the 1780s, was probably never said by her. The phrase is apocryphal, going back at least one hundred years prior to Marie-Antoinette's arrival in France. The queen is known to have shown many acts of kindness toward the poor and underprivileged during her reign.

The queen never dressed as a milkmaid or a shepherdess at the Hameau (Hamlet) in the gardens of the Petit Trianon. She did, however, play such roles on the stage of her little theater.

Marie-Antoinette did not hold orgies at the Petit Trianon, lesbian or otherwise; in fact, she was a bit of a prude. She did not even drink alcohol.

Although known for her fondness for diamonds in her younger years, she never owned or wanted to own the massive diamond necklace stolen by a group of swindlers that was at the center of a scandal of 1785–1786. Yet the "Affair of the Diamond Necklace" permanently tarnished the queen's reputation and has been seen as a major contributory cause of the French Revolution. Despite the queen's innocence in the affair somehow her enemies managed to promote the idea that it was the queen's fault.

"I have ever believed that had there been no queen, there would have been no revolution," said Thomas Jefferson, former American ambassador to France. Jefferson blamed the queen's extravagance for the bankruptcy of France's treasury, thus avoiding admitting that it had more to do with France's generous support for the American struggle for independence.

During her trial in October 1793 Marie-Antoinette was accused of sexually abusing her son, the dauphin. The queen bravely denied any unseemly actions toward her son, appealing to the mothers in the court. This was the only moment when she won sympathy from the courtroom in her final hours.

Fig. 23 Elisabeth Louise Vigée Le Brun (1755–1842), *Marie-Antoinette Seated in a Blue Mantle and White Skirt*, 1788. Oil on canvas. Musée du Château de Versailles

This was the last official portrait of the queen. The artist Vigée Le Brun later recalled that Marie-Antoinette "had irregular features; the oval and straight face of her family peculiar to the Austrians. She had small eyes that were almost blue; . . . a fine and pretty nose, small mouth although the lips were a bit large. Her most remarkable feature was her complexion. I have never seen such brilliance, and brilliant is the word; as her skin was so translucent that it had no shadows."

From Archduchess of Austria to Dauphine of France

Fig. 24 Martin van Meytens the Younger (1695–1770), *The Austrian Imperial Family in 1756*, 1756. Oil on canvas. Musée du Château de Versailles

The portrait shows the extensive family of Empress Maria-Theresa and Emperor Francis I. Marie-Antoinette is the baby in the cradle.

"Surely never lighted on this orb . . . a more delightful vision."

EDMUND BURKE, 1793

Marie-Antoinette was the fifteenth child of Empress Maria-Theresa of Austria and Emperor Francis Stephen of Lorraine. Brought up in a comfortable atmosphere in Vienna, she had a happy childhood in a large family (fig. 24). At the age of fourteen she was betrothed to the heir to the French throne to seal a political alliance between France and Austria. The two countries had been traditional enemies in the eighteenth century, and the young princess was essentially a pawn in a political game played by her mother and Louis XV (fig. 25).

Married by proxy in Vienna, she made the long journey to France in a protracted ceremonial procession. She was received rapturously at Versailles, pleasing King Louis XV with her fresh looks, her grace, and her charm. She was married to Louis XVI in a second ceremony at Versailles on May 16, 1770. Marie-Antoinette was shocked by the coldness of the French royal family and the relentless and rigid etiquette of Versailles. She wrote to her mother in 1770, "I apply my rouge and wash my hands in front of everyone," dismayed by the ritual of getting dressed in front of her court.

Fig. 25 Joseph Ducreux (1735–1802), *The Archduchess Maria Antonia of Austria*, 1769. Pastel on parchment. Musée du Château de Versailles

Empress Maria-Theresa sent this pastel portrait to Louis XV before the marriage of her daughter to the dauphin.

Fig. 26 Jewel casket of the dauphine, 1770, Martin Carlin, cabinetmaker. Tulipwood and sycamore veneers, Sèvres porcelain plaques, and gilt-bronze mounts. Musée du Château de Versailles

Given to Marie-Antoinette as a wedding present, this container for her jewels is mounted with expensive porcelain plaques. The drawer contains a desk.

JOHANN GEORG WEIKERT (1745 OR
1743–1799)

CAT. 1 *Représentation à Schönbrunn
par les archiduchesses d'Autriche du
divertissement "Il Parnaso confuso,"
le 24 janvier 1765 (Performance at
Schönbrunn by the Archduchesses
of Austria of "Il Parnaso confuso,"
24 January 1765), 1778*

Monogrammed and dated lower right: *W.f.* (1) 778; Oil
on canvas; 9 ft. 5¾ in. × 6 ft. 10⅛ in. (2.89 × 2.085 m);
Inv. MV3944

CAT. 2 *Représentation à Schönbrunn par
les archiducs Ferdinand et Maximilien
d'Autriche, et l'archiduchesse Marie-
Antoinette du ballet-pantomime "Le
Triomphe de l'Amour," le 24 janvier 1765
(Performance at Schönbrunn by the
Archdukes Ferdinand and Maximilien
of Austria and the Archduchess Marie-
Antoinette of the Ballet-Pantomime "The
Triumph of Love," 24 January 1765), 1778*

Oil on canvas; 9 ft. 4⅝ in. × 6 ft. 11 in. (2.86 × 2.11 m);
Inv. MV3945

PROVENANCE: Paintings commissioned in 1778 by Marie-
Antoinette for the dining room of the Petit Trianon, to
replace Doyen's *La pêche (Fishing)* and Hallé's *La vendange
(The Grape Harvest)*; according to Jallut (1955, p. 26), both
mentioned as at the Grand Trianon on August 18, 1792;
installed by Louis-Philippe in the Galeries Historiques at
Versailles; exhibited in 1867 at the Petit Trianon; both canvases removed from the dining room in 1939

BIBL.: Desjardins 1885, pp. 163–164; Jallut 1955, p. 26;
Brière-Misme 1968, pp. 223–224; Salmon, Bordeaux,
2005, pp. 80–84, nos. 10 and 11, repr.

Commissioned by Marie-Antoinette in 1778, these paintings are copies of canvases undoubtedly painted in 1765 by a collabora-tor of Martin van Meytens, depicting members of the imperial fam-ily performing at Schönbrunn in honor of the second marriage of Joseph II, to Marie-Josephine-Antoinette of Bavaria, on January 24 of that year. In the first painting, the archduchesses perform a scene from Gluck's opera *Il Parnaso confuso.* Accompanied by the arch-duke Leopold, who played basso continuo with the orchestra, they acted the parts of Apollo and the Muses. The second painting shows the archduke Maximilian as Cupid; his brother Ferdinand and sis-ter Marie-Antoinette dance alongside him. On the left are the little princesses of Clary and Auersperg, their mirror-images on the right are their brothers and the landgrave of Furstemberg. They are per-forming "The Triumph of Love," the ballet-pantomime that closed the opera.

The two paintings, magnificent assemblages of portraits of people dear to the queen's heart, brought back memories of her childhood. The painting that featured her also celebrated her talents for dance and music.

On January 5, 1778, Empress Maria-Theresa wrote her daughter Marie-Antoinette:

> Mercy [Mercy-Argenteau, the Austrian ambassador to France] sent me the measurements for a painting that you would wish for Trianon; it is the opera played at the Emperor's wedding festivities. It gives me the greatest pleasure in the world to serve you; but I need a clarification: there are two: one the opera, the other the ballet with a certain little queen [Marie-Antoinette] and her two brothers. I think the one you want is the latter, or perhaps both. You will be served; but in that case I need measurements for the second painting as well, to know what side the light is on, if it is to be a painting or to serve as a tapestry to be attached to the wall.

Marie-Antoinette replied on January 15:

> My dear Mamma overwhelms me with her kindness with regard to the paintings; I would never have dared ask for them, though they would give me the greatest pleasure in the world. . . . I am not sending with this courier the measurements to my dear Mamma, because the concierge of the Trianon, where I mean to place the paintings, is away.

> Shortly thereafter, Pierre-Charles Bonnefoy du Plan, the Trianon's concierge, returned, and Marie-Antoinette sent the dimensions to her mother. On February 12, 1779, Mercy-Argenteau delivered the two much-anticipated works to the queen.

Xavier Salmon

CAT. 1 **WEIKERT** *Représentation à Schönbrunn par les archiduchesses d'Autriche du*
divertissement "Il Parnaso confuso." le 24 janvier 1765
(Performance at Schönbrunn by the Archduchesses of Austria of "Il Parnaso confuso."
24 January 1765)

CAT. 2 WEIKERT *Représentation à Schönbrunn par les archiducs Ferdinand et Maximilien d'Autriche, et l'archiduchesse Marie-Antoinette du ballet-pantomime "Le Triomphe de l'Amour," le 24 janvier 1765*
(Performance at Schönbrunn by the Archdukes Ferdinand and Maximilian of Austria and the Archduchess Marie-Antoinette of the Ballet-Pantomime "The Triumph of Love," 24 January 1765)

CAT. 3 Salver with the arms
of the French Dauphin and
Marie-Antoinette, Archduchess
of Austria, 1769–1770

JOHANN-WILHELM DAMMAN, EXECUTED BY
WILHELM MICHAEL RAUNER, AUGSBURG,
GERMANY

Inscription on the pedestal: *Fait par Guillaume Michel
Rauner à Augsbourg*; Hallmarks: the letter *T* crowned with
a pinecone, for Augsburg in 1769–1771 [Seling, no. 255];
IWD for Johann Wilhelm Damman, [Seling, no. 2387];
Rauner's mark; Silver-gilt; 3⅛ × 13⅜ × 10¼ in. (8 × 34 ×
26 cm); Inv. v3570

PROVENANCE: Collection of Marie-Antoinette; sale
March 15, 1880 (Florence, Palazzo di San Donato,
no. 1309); Niel Collection; Acquired by the Château de
Versailles in 1955, gift of the comte and comtesse Niel

BIBL.: Baumstark, Seling, 1994, p. XIII; Hans, Kobe-Tokyo,
2002, no. 79; Hans, Bordeaux, 2005, no. 54

The wedding of Marie-Antoinette to the dauphin Louis-Auguste took place in great state at the chapel of Versailles on May 16, 1770. This piece of silver was ordered for the occasion from the Augsburg goldsmith Johann Wilhelm Damman. The purpose of this salver was for presenting objects such as the princess's gloves during the ceremony.

The scene on the plateau of the salver shows an allegory of the wedding of the dauphin of France to the archduchess of Austria. The figures in antique costume represent France and Austria, their hands united and lit by the torches of Hymen, who presides over the marriage. Putti on either side support shields with the arms of Austria on the left and France on the right. In front are dolphins, emblems of the dauphin of France.

Pierre-Xavier Hans

CAT. 4 Coffer with the arms of Marie-Antoinette, Dauphine of France, between 1770 and 1774

WORKSHOP OF ANTOINE LANSON, CASEMAKER

Marked with the letters *A* and *L* on either side of a rooster, for Antoine Lanson; Wood covered in red morocco, stamped gilding, gilt-bronze mounts; 21 × 29⅛ × 19¼ in. (53.3 × 74 × 49 cm); Inv. v2367

PROVENANCE: Acquired by the Château de Versailles in 1911, gift of the marquise de Ligneris

BIBL.: Hans, Kobe-Tokyo, 2002, no. 86; Hans, Bordeaux, 2005, no. 52

Fig. 27 After Elisabeth Louise Vigée Le Brun (1755–1842), *Marie-Antoinette de Lorraine d'Autriche, Reine de France*, 1828. Etching and engraving on chine collé. Fine Arts Museums of San Francisco, 25771

Queen of France

"Lord guide us and protect us, for we are too young to rule" was the phrase reputedly uttered by Louis XVI and Marie-Antoinette upon learning of the death of Louis XV and their accession in May 1774. Marie-Antoinette was just eighteen and her husband was nearly twenty years old. The couple followed the traditions at Versailles laid down by Louis XIV one hundred years earlier. Marie-Antoinette performed the public ceremonies expected of a French queen—dressing, holding audiences, and eating in public—but she alienated influential members of the court and the royal family. Finding the antiquated etiquette stifling, the young queen looked for pursuits to divert her, including horseback riding, for which she was much criticized by her own mother, who believed it might imperil her chance of having children. Louis XVI was ill prepared to rule. He was shy and retiring, preferring to hunt and to work in his locksmiths' shop, and he did not know how to have marital relations. It has been suggested that, in addition to her extreme youth, Marie-Antoinette's frustrations about her childless marriage may have prompted her frivolous and hectic social life in the first years of her reign.

JEAN-BAPTISTE ANDRÉ GAUTIER-DAGOTY
(1740–1786)

CAT. 5 *Marie-Antoinette en grand habit
de cour (Marie-Antoinette in Court
Dress)*, 1775

Oil on canvas; 63 × 50⅜ in. (160 × 128 cm); Inv.
MV 8062

PROVENANCE: Commissioned by Marie-Antoinette and
displayed in the *galerie des glaces* (Hall of Mirrors) at Versailles on July 27, 1775; given by Marie-Antoinette to Prince
Georg Adam von Starhemberg in 1777; Starhemberg Collection; gift to the Château de Versailles from Commander
Paul-Louis Weiller in 1954

BIBL.: Salmon 1993–1994, pp. 98–101, 202–203, repr.

autier-Dagoty received his most important commission, Marie-
Antoinette's portrait, in 1775. Completed in July of that year, the
work had been painted "from life in keeping with the orders received."
It was immediately shown in the *galerie des glaces* (Hall of Mirrors) at
Versailles. Despite its official quality—demonstrated by the profusion
of fleurs-de-lis, the royal crown on the cushion, and the presence of
the bust of Louis XVI that Minerva holds in the background—the
image failed to please. Madame Campan wrote: "The most worthless
artists were given the honor of painting her; a full-length painting of
her in all her royal pomp was exhibited in the gallery at Versailles.
This painting, meant for the court at Vienna and painted by a man
who does not deserve to be named, disgusted all people of taste." Sen-
sitive to the criticisms aroused by her portrait, the queen in the end
decided not to send it to her mother, Maria-Theresa, as she had originally intended. In 1777 she gave it to Prince von Starhemberg. As for
Gautier-Dagoty, he derived some fame for having been allowed to
portray the queen. To commemorate the event, he painted a gouache
depicting the sitting in the queen's bedchamber at Versailles during
which he set down her features (fig. 28).

Xavier Salmon

Fig. 28 Jean-Baptiste André Gautier-Dagoty (1740–1786),
*Gautier-Dagoty Painting the Queen in Her Bedchamber at
Versailles*, ca. 1775. Gouache on paper. Musée du Château
de Versailles

The artist is in the process of painting the queen's portrait
on a large oval canvas (see cat. 5). A fascinating impression of a morning in the queen's bedchamber at Versailles,
this gouache shows the queen playing the harp dressed in
a peignoir. A woman on the left reads; two women—one
perhaps Rose Bertin, Marie-Antoinette's *marchande de
modes*—present some feathers for headdresses on the
queen's dressing table by her silver-gilt-framed mirror. By
the great bed, with its *gros de Tours* hangings, hairdressers
with combs in their hair work on a wig or headdress.

CAT. 6 *Bust of Marie-Antoinette*, ca. 1775

ROYAL PORCELAIN MANUFACTORY,
SÈVRES, AFTER LOUIS-SIMON BOIZOT
(1743–1809)

Hard-paste porcelain biscuitware; 12⅜ (exclusive of
base) × 7⅞ in. (31.5 × 20 cm); Inv. MV 7784

PROVENANCE: Acquired by the Château de Versailles in
the nineteenth century

BIBL.: Bourgeois 1907, pp. 406–407, repr. fig. 2; Piquenard
2001, pp. 83–85, repr.; Salmon, Kobe-Tokyo, 2002, p. 228,
no. 69, repr. p. 141; Salmon, Bordeaux, 2005, p. 77, no. 8

The sculptor Louis-Simon Boizot was named director of the sculpture workshops at the Sèvres porcelain factory in 1773, when Marie-Antoinette was still dauphine. After she came to the throne in 1774 she commissioned Boizot to make busts of the royal couple.

The model was executed in biscuit porcelain, which was unglazed and very close to marble in its whiteness and fine grain. Two sizes were produced: a smaller one, shown here; and a larger example, which was a little more than 26¾ inches (68 cm) in height.

If not the first, this bust was one of the first made of the young queen. It showed the natural grace and dignity for which she was noted by many of her contemporaries. The details of the discreet diadem crowning her high hairstyle as well as the mantle lined with ermine acknowledged her royal status. Boizot's talents should be credited with creating a faithful image of the queen, following her features closely, but without hiding her faults.

The model must have pleased the queen because she sent an example in biscuit porcelain to her mother, Empress Maria-Theresa, at the beginning of 1775; she also named Boizot her portraitist in sculpture.

Bertrand Rondot

ATTRIBUTED TO LOUIS-SIMON BOIZOT (1743–1809)

CAT. 7 *Profile of Marie-Antoinette*, 1774

Inscribed on the back: *Marie-Antoinette / josephe-jeanne d'autriche. / Reine de france / 1774*; Marble; 21 × 15¾ × 2¾ in. (53.5 × 40 × 7 cm); Inv. MV 6306

PROVENANCE: Inventoried at Versailles in 1824, 1840, and 1846; entered into the inventories between 1938 and 1940; returned to the Château de Versailles in 1974, after a period in storage at the Louvre

BIBL.: Vandalle 2002, p. 227, no. 68, repr. p. 140; Salmon, Bordeaux, 2005, p. 76, no. 7, repr.; Scherf 2001, p. 87, no. 240 repr.

Louis-Auguste Brun, called Brun de Versoix (1758–1815)

CAT. 8 *Marie-Antoinette on Horseback*, n.d.

Oil on canvas; 23⅝ × 26 in. (60 × 66 cm); Inv. MV 5718

PROVENANCE: Collection of the painter's descendants; gift to the Château de Versailles in 1912 through the Société des Amis de Versailles

BIBL.: de Herdt and de La Rochefoucauld 1986, p. 99, no. 10, repr. p. 38, fig. 11 (with detailed bibl.); Salmon, Bordeaux, 2005, pp. 85–86, no. 12, repr. 10

CAT. 9 Coffee Service with Portraits of
the Royal Family, 1778–1779

Paris, Rue Saint-Denis Factory; Porcelain; Inv. V6053

A. Coffee pot with lid [Louis XVI and
Marie-Antoinette]

7½ in. (19 cm)

B. Sugar box with lid [Comte and
Comtesse d'Artois]

Marked with a lowercase *h* in blue for Hannong;
4⅜ in. (11 cm)

C. Milk jug with lid [Comte and
Comtesse de Provence]

Marked with a lowercase *h* in blue for Hannong;
5¼ in. (13.5 cm)

D. Three cups and three saucers
[Madame Clotilde, Madame Elizabeth,
and Madame Louise]

Marked with a lowercase *h* in blue for Hannong;
2¾ × diam. 5¾ in. (7 × 14.5 cm)

PROVENANCE: Purchased by the Château de Versailles
in 2004

BIBL.: Plinval de Guillebon 1995, pp. 136–138; Hans,
Bordeaux, 2005, pp. 159–161, no. 59

This partial coffee service displays portraits of the various members of the royal family at the time Louis XVI and Marie-Antoinette came to the throne. The royal couple are shown on the coffee pot, Louis' brother the comte de Provence (later Louis XVIII) and the comtesse de Provence are on the milk jug, and Louis' other brother, the comte d'Artois (later Charles X), and the comtesse d'Artois are on the sugar box. Two of the cups show Louis' sisters: Madame Clotilde, queen of Sardinia, and Madame Elisabeth. The other cup shows Madame Louise, Louis XVI's aunt, who became a Carmelite nun in 1770. The service seems to be missing pieces with portraits of the king's other aunts, known as Mesdames Tantes, Adélaïde, Sophie, and Victoire, who would complete the immediate family circle.

Pierre-Xavier Hans

The Queen's Taste: Preciousness and Elegance

Fig. 29 The *cabinet de la méridienne*, Marie-Antoinette's boudoir at Versailles. Redecorated for the queen in 1782, this tiny octagonal room was recast to give an impression of richness, preciousness, and upholstered comfort.

Bought for Marie-Antoinette in 1782, this masterpiece of the bronzeworker Gouthière was made for the duc d'Aumont in 1774–1775. It is an iconic example of the finest French decorative arts made during the neoclassical era. The queen probably displayed it in her *cabinet doré* at Versailles.

The queen instigated many schemes for the interiors of the royal palaces, calling on the Garde-Meuble, the office responsible for royal furnishing and decoration. The royal designers and architects transformed her apartments to reflect the queen's particular taste for preciousness, elegance, and femininity. Her small private rooms had light color schemes enlivened with gilding, and elaborate upholstery. Their delicate, classical designs, executed with astonishing craftsmanship and in meticulous detail, made a dazzling impression. For furnishings, she commissioned small pieces veneered with elaborate marquetry veneers of exotic woods and mounted with intricate gilt-bronze ornament. The *cabinet intérieur,* her study, was her most sumptuous private room at Versailles (fig. 17). There she displayed her art collection, including rare Japanese lacquer inherited from her mother and a precious hardstone vase mounted in gilt bronze, a masterpiece of decorative arts by Pierre Gouthière (fig. 30). As an act of patronage she also commissioned porcelain from the royal factory at Sèvres, including a large dinner service, which was decorated with her favorite floral motifs (cat. 13).

CAT. 10 Sofa (canapé à la turque), 1779

JACQUES GONDOIN (1737–1818),
DESIGNER

FRANÇOIS-TOUSSAINT FOLIOT (CALLED
FRANÇOIS II) (1748–AFTER 1808), CARVER

WIDOW BABEL (DATES UNKNOWN) AND
WIDOW BARDOU (DATES UNKNOWN),
GILDERS

ALTERED(?) BY GEORGES JACOB, MASTER
IN 1765

Stamped: *G. Jacob* under the seat rail; Beech, carved, gilded, and (later) painted; upholstery (modern); 39½ × 90½ × 31¾ in. (100.3 × 229.9 × 80.7 cm); Fine Arts Museums of San Francisco, Roscoe and Margaret Oakes Collection, 57.23.5

PROVENANCE: Commissioned for Marie-Antoinette's *cabinet intérieur*; Gouverneur Morris, ca. 1794; Mrs. Cornelius Vanderbilt, her sale Plaza Art Galleries, New York, January 9, 1954; Dalva Bothers, New York; bt. 1956 by Margaret H. and Roscoe F. Oakes, by whom given to the M. H. de Young Memorial Museum, San Francisco, 1957

BIBL.: Verlet 1963, pp. 162–168; Rieder 1980, pp. 47–54

This sofa was originally designed as part of a suite for the queen's new decorative scheme for the *cabinet intérieur* (private study) of 1779. It was conceived by Jacques Gondoin, the *dessinateur du mobilier de la Couronne* (royal furniture designer), in the rich version of the neoclassical style that he was using in his designs for the furnishings and decorations of the Marie-Antoinette's private apartments. The queen's private study was redesigned as an entity, with the furniture integrated into the scheme. Relatively small and light in color, the room was decorated with many mirrors and with rich figured silk wall panels, drapery, and upholstery. The rails and back of the sofa's frame are carved with massed heads of flowers, one of the queen's favorite motifs. The curved arms are formed as scrolls emerging from horns of plenty. The latter form is an emblem of fecundity, a subject dear to Marie-Antoinette's heart as both a mother and a queen who was expected to bear children for a future Bourbon dynasty. It is probably no accident that the arms also seem to represent Cupid's bow.

The sofa was refused upon delivery, probably due to a change made to the place it was intended for in the study. At ninety inches, it is far too long for the mirrored niche that is indicated on Gondoin's plan as being six *pieds* (six French feet, roughly seventy-six inches).[1] It is not certain whether it was covered in the sumptuous silk designed by Gondoin for this scheme (cat. 11). The sofa was probably used elsewhere in the queen's private apartments. The queen's favorite *menuisier* (chair-frame maker), Georges Jacob, whose name is stamped under the seat rail, must have repaired this sofa, possibly cutting it down to its present length. It was also later decorated differently from the rest of the suite, which is entirely gilded, as the flower heads, feet, and arms have been painted in a grayish white.

Gouverneur Morris (1752–1816), who was American ambassador to the French state, purchased the sofa at the time of the Revolutionary sales; however, it does not seem to be recorded at Morrisania, his New York home. It is not known when the sofa came to be in the collection of Mrs. Cornelius Vanderbilt.

Martin Chapman

NOTE
1. Eleanor Tolfree, "Le mobilier de Marie-Antoinette à la Wallace Collection," *Versalia*, no. 9 (2006): p. 156.

CAT. 11 Panel of silk designed for the queen's *cabinet intérieur* (private study), Versailles, ca. 1779

JEAN CHARTON (MASTER IN 1733), SILK MANUFACTURER, LYON, AFTER JACQUES GONDOIN (1737–1818), DESIGNER FOR THE GARDE-MEUBLE DE LA COURONNE

Silk lampas, satin ground applied with embroidered silk chenille medallions; 67 × 20½ in. (1.7 m × 52 cm); Inv. v3924

PROVENANCE: Acquired by the Château de Versailles in 1963, Chaigneau gift

BIBL.: Coural and Arizzoli-Clémentel 1988, pp. 116–117, no. 24, repr. p. 41; Baulez 2001, pp. 29–41; Jallut 1964, pp. 289–353; Hans, Kobe-Tokyo, 2002, no. 78; Hans, Bordeaux, 2005, pp. 124–135, no. 41

CAT. 12 Marie-Antoinette's collection of Japanese lacquer

A. Box in the shape of a dog lying on a low table

Japan, 18th century; Lacquer; Both pieces: 6⅛ × 9 × 4¾ in. (15.5 × 23 × 12 cm); box: 3¾ × 6¼ × 4½ in. (9.5 × 16 × 11.5 cm); low table (6 × 23 × 12.7 cm); Inv. MR 380-90

B. Box in the shape of two overlapping fans

Japan, 18th century; Lacquer; 1 × 5¼ × 3½ in. (2.5 × 13.3 × 8.8 cm); Inv. MR380-7

PROVENANCE OF A AND B: Collection of Marie-Antoinette; exhibited in her Cabinet Doré at Versailles; October 10, 1789, collection inventoried then sent to Paris; 1794, transferred to the Musée du Louvre; 1965, gift of most of the collection to the Château de Versailles

BIBL.: Nagashima 1999, vol. 22, pp. 25–66 and IV–V; Kopplin 2001

C. Box with the silhouette of Hotei, god of Good Fortune

Japan, 18th century; Lacquer; 1¾ × 4¼ × 3⅜ in. (4.5 × 10.7 × 8.5 cm); Inv. MR380-34

PROVENANCE: Randon de Boisset, sale of February 1777

Marie-Antoinette was enthusiastic about collecting Japanese lacquerwares, which she exhibited in her private study, the *cabinet doré* at Versailles. Her mother, Empress Maria-Theresa of Austria, bequeathed to her a group of fifty boxes in lacquer, which arrived at Versailles in May 1781. Marie-Antoinette further enriched her collection by buying some exceptional pieces from dealers in Paris.

CAT. 13 Pieces from Marie-Antoinette's
service riche en couleurs et riche en or
("Richly Colored and Richly Gilded"
dinner service), 1784

Royal Porcelain Manufactory, Sèvres; Mark *LL* and date-letters *GG* for the year 1784; Marks of the painters Barrat, Butteux, Cornailles, Fumez, Levé, Micaud, Niquet, Pfeiffer, Rosset, and Taillandier; Marks of the gilders Chauveaux, Foinet, Prévost, and Vincent; Soft- and hard-paste porcelain; Inv. v5734

PROVENANCE: Commissioned by Marie-Antoinette; dispersed during the Revolution; purchased by the Château de Versailles by preemption at a public sale in 1993

BIBL.: Baulez 1994, pp. 78–79; Hans, Bordeaux, 2005, no. 57

A. Two dinner plates

Marks of the painters Niquet, Rosset, Cornailles, Taillandier, Barrat, and Levé; 1⅛ × diam. 9¼ in. (2.8 × 23.5 cm); Inv. v5734 / 36–37

B. Crenellated wine-glass cooler

Mark of the painter, Pfeiffer; Mark of the gilder, Prévost; 5⅜ × 11⅞ × 8⅛ in. (13.5 × 30 × 20.8 cm) Inv. v5734 / 35

C. Two butter dishes

Mark of the painter, Micaud; Mark of the gilder, Foinet; 3⅛ × diam. 7⅞ in. (8 × 19.9 cm); Inv. v5734 / 17–18

D. Round lobed plate

1½ × diam. 11¼ in. (3.7 × 28.5 cm); Inv. v5734 / 2

E. Round plate

1⅜ × diam. 11⅞ in. (4 × 30.2 cm); Inv. v5734 / 6

F. Two wine-glass coolers

Mark of the painter, Niquet; Mark of the gilder, Chauveaux; 4¼ × diam. 4⅝ in. (10.8 × 11.8 cm); Inv. v5734 / 27–28

At the beginning of 1784, Marie-Antoinette ordered from the Royal Porcelain Manufactory at Sèvres a dinner service that may have been intended for her apartment in the Tuileries Palace. The design was decided upon in January. Several painters from the factory worked simultaneously on models decorated "with a rich border," and by early February the painters' designs were ready for the queen's review. The artist of the pattern she selected remains unknown. Antoine Régnier, director of the factory, told the comte d'Angiviller, *surintendant des bâtiments*, on February 21 that the queen had kept the model for a plate and ordered a complete service. In response to the queen's impatience, Régnier mobilized the artisans of the factory. On March 27 he indicated that the gilding of the pieces was beginning, and on May 3 he announced that the work was nearly completed. However, on June 22 Louis XVI offered the service made for the queen to the king of Sweden, Gustav III, on his visit to France. Therefore, Sèvres had to make a second service, with a very similar composition and in an identical pattern, in order to fulfill the queen's commission. This service, with its "richly colored and richly gilded" decoration, was delivered to Versailles on August 26.

Each of the two services consisted of 239 pieces. The service delivered to the queen included two *pots à oille* worth 600 *livres* (pounds) each; two tureens with their plates, at the same price; fifteen soup plates at 36 *livres* each; twelve single, double, and triple salt cellars; six salad bowls in two sizes; twenty-four large plates, oval and round, of different sizes; mustard pots; sauce boats; gravy boats with their stands; butter dishes; radish plates; and egg cups. The dessert portion of the service included seventy-two dinner plates at 36 *livres* each; sixteen compote dishes at 48 *livres* each; sixteen wine-glass coolers at 60 *livres* each; six wine-bottle coolers at 198 *livres* each; two wine coolers for half-bottles at 156 *livres* each; two oval wine-bottle coolers at 156 *livres*; and two *verrières* (crenellated wine-glass coolers) at 264 *livres* each (Arch. Manu. Sèvres Vy 9, f° 141 v°). The service cost 16,350 *livres*.

The service is decorated with a wide border, which features alternating cornflowers and roses framed by a very delicate garland of myrtle. The border also has medallions of white pearls enclosing a pansy. This service, which iterates the queen's favorite decorative repertory of pearls and flowers, is the most opulent of the services that Sèvres produced for the queen. Marie-Antoinette's and Gustav III's services were dispersed, Marie-Antoinette's during the Revolution. The pieces on exhibit belong to a set of forty-eight from Marie-Antoinette's service.

Pierrre-Xavier Hans

Motherhood

Marie-Antoinette's primary role was to seal the future of the Bourbon dynasty by having children. Due to lack of sex education, Marie-Antoinette and Louis XVI did not have children for seven years. The queen's brother, the emperor Joseph II, made a special visit in 1777 for the purpose of instructing them, and Marie-Antoinette had her first child the following year. She settled into as much of a conventional family life as was possible within the rigid formalities of the court. The queen's own childhood had been a happy one, and motherhood brought her great joy. She was an attentive parent and was much concerned with the upbringing and education of her children (figs. 31, 32). However, her happiness was not to last: two of her four children died very young. Her daughter Madame Sophie, born in 1786, lived only eleven months, and the highly anticipated first dauphin, Louis-Joseph-Xavier-François, died of tuberculosis at not quite nine years of age, just as the Revolution was breaking out in July 1789.

Fig. 31 Adolf Ulrich Wertmüller (1751–1811), *Queen Marie-Antoinette Walking with Her Children near the Temple of Love in the Gardens of the Petit Trianon*, 1785. Oil on canvas. Nationalmuseum, Stockholm, Sweden

Fig. 32 Elisabeth Louise Vigée Le Brun (1755–1842), *Marie-Antoinette and Her Children*, 1787. Oil on canvas. Musée du château de Versailles

ELISABETH LOUISE VIGÉE LE BRUN
(1755–1842)

CAT. 14 *Madame Royale and Her Brother,
the Dauphin, Louis-Joseph-Xavier
François, 1784*

Signed and dated lower right: *L. Le Brun f. 1784*; Oil on canvas; 52 × 37 in. (1.32 m × 94 cm); Inv. MV 3907

PROVENANCE: Commissioned by Marie-Antoinette; exhibited at the Salon in 1785 (no. 85); mentioned as at the Musée du Louvre from 1818; sent from the Louvre to the Château de Versailles in September 1899

BIBL.: Vigée Le Brun 1835–1837, p. 332; Baillio 1982, pp. 49–51, no. 13, repr.; Salmon, Bordeaux, 2005, pp. 102–103, no. 24, repr.

For this painting of 1784, Vigée Le Brun borrowed François-Hubert Drouais's favorite formula of the 1760s of a double portrait of children in a landscape. Maurice Blot's 1786 print of this painting was, in fact, designed as a pendant of the one made in 1763 after Drouais's portrait *Le comte d'Artois et Madame Clotilde* (Château de Versailles, Inv. MV3898). Vigée Le Brun very clearly drew her inspiration from her predecessor's painting. The royal children display the same tender gestures as the children in Drouais's portrait, with the elder resting her left hand on her brother's shoulder.

Though the two paintings differ in their details, they both integrate the children into a natural environment. To mitigate his painting's "official" quality, Drouais inserted into the comte d'Artois' hand a fistful of grass that lures the billy goat bearing his sister. Similarly, Vigée Le Brun placed a nest of baby birds in the center foreground. In addition, by eschewing strict frontal poses for the sitters, she endowed the painting with grace and sensitivity, characteristics that were typical of the artist's work and contributed to her great success as a portraitist. Madame Royale gazes down affectionately at her brother, who looks out the viewer.

This double portrait was well received at the 1785 Salon. In 1789 Vigée Le Brun executed a replica of the painting (ex-collection Roberto Polo).

Xavier Salmon

The Queen's Unpopularity: Mounting Scandals

P ublic opinion turned firmly against the queen in the 1780s, fueled by an active underground press of pamphlets and prints of her imagined licentious exploits. By 1789 the queen could do little right in the eyes of the people. In the court circles at Versailles, the queen alienated those whose support she needed most by not adhering strictly to etiquette or precedent. Seen as being from the enemy country of Austria and not acting in France's best interests, she was dubbed the *Autrichienne* (Austrian bitch), even by her husband's maiden aunts, Mesdames Tantes, who were supposedly her friends.

Marie-Antoinette came to be regarded widely as frivolous, as a result of projects such as the building of her pleasure gardens at the Petit Trianon. The debacle over her portrait by Vigée Le Brun depicting the queen in a light muslin dress offended her conservative critics in 1783, but her unpopularity reached a new level with the scandal of the "Affair of the Diamond Necklace" in 1785–1786. This was a successful plot to swindle an elaborate diamond necklace worth 1.8 million *livres* (French pounds) from the royal jewelers, Boehmer and Bassenge. Although the queen never had any interest in the necklace, public opinion held otherwise, believing somehow that she was behind the plot, and her reputation was permanently ruined.

ELISABETH LOUISE VIGÉE LE BRUN
(1755–1842)

CAT. 15 *Marie-Antoinette en gaulle*
(Marie-Antoinette in a Muslin Dress),
1783

Oil on canvas; 36¾ × 31⅛ in. (93.5 × 79 cm); Collection of
the Hessische Hausstiftung, Germany, WO B 8250

PROVENANCE: Given by Marie-Antoinette to her childhood friend Princess Louise of Hesse-Darmstadt

BIBL.: Sheriff 2003, pp. 45–73; Ribero 1995, pp. 70–71;
Vigée Le Brun 1986; Weber 2006, pp. 156–163

One of the most beautiful images of the queen, this portrait of
Marie-Antoinette caused a furor when it was exhibited at the
Salon in 1783. Shown in an informal pose, the queen wears the infa-
mous *gaulle*, later known as a *chemise à la reine*, a dress of light summer muslin simply tied with a sash at the waist. Worn with a straw
hat decorated with feathers and ribbons, the *gaulle* was the queen's
preferred style of dress when away from court at the Petit Trianon.
The queen and her close intimates, the duchesse de Polignac among
them, set the fashion for these muslin dresses in the early 1780s;
even the queen's rival, the comtesse Du Barry, the former mistress
of Louis XV, was painted by Vigée Le Brun wearing the *gaulle*. However, conservative opinion was outraged that such a casual image of
the queen would be shown at the Salon, and some critics purposely
mistook her dress for her underwear and connoted it with indecency.
Vigée Le Brun responded to this criticism by removing the portrait
from the Salon and replacing it with a more conventional one. In this
subsequent version, *Marie Antoinette "à la rose,"* the queen is painted
in a similar pose holding a rose, but wearing a more formal silk dress
(cat. 16). The irony of this scandal is that this type of light muslin
dress would become popular under the Directory in the 1790s, when
it was seen as the very height of Revolutionary taste.

Martin Chapman

ELISABETH LOUISE VIGÉE LE BRUN
(1755–1842)

CAT. 16 *Marie-Antoinette "à la rose,"*
1783

Oil on canvas; 44½ × 34¼ in. (1.13 m × 87 cm);
Inv. MV3893

PROVENANCE: Entered the Château de Versailles under
Louis-Philippe

BIBL.: Salmon, *Marie-Antoinette*, 2005, pp. 117–118, repr.

On May 31, 1783, Elisabeth Louise Vigée Le Brun was approved by the Académie royale de peinture et sculpture and received as a member at the same sitting, thanks to the queen's influence. Vigée Le Brun also exhibited for the first time at the Salon of that year. Among the works she showed was a new portrait of Marie-Antoinette. The queen was portrayed wearing a *chemise* and a straw hat (cat. 15). Her outfit was very fashionable at the time: the casual muslin dress was a style that may have originated in Creole costume from the West Indies and was adapted in Paris by the modiste Rose Bertin.

When the painting was shown to the public it immediately created a scandal. The author of the *Mémoires secrets pour servir à l'histoire de la République des Lettres en France* wrote:

> Madame Lebrun exhibited three portraits of the royal family, those of the Queen, of Monsieur, of Madame. Both princesses wear a chemise, a costume recently invented by the women. Many people have found it unsuitable for these august personages to be displayed in public in a garment reserved for inside their palaces, it is to be presumed that the artist was permitted to do so and would not have herself taken such a liberty.

This was all the more insidious since, according to the author of the memoir, only the queen could have given her authorization to appear so costumed. The indecency of the costume in the end caused the painting to be withdrawn from the Salon. Vigée Le Brun quickly painted another portrait, in which the queen was depicted in exactly the same pose, but wearing a classic dress of blue-gray—a color known as "London chimney soot"—in a much less controversial style. The painting paid homage to French fashion and implicitly expressed Marie-Antoinette's support for the silk weavers of Lyon. It was an instant success, and Vigée Le Brun was commissioned to paint several replicas, including the famous example at Versailles.

Xavier Salmon

White sapphires, metal; Inv. v5925

PROVENANCE: Acquired by the Château de Versailles in 1963, gift of Madame Laubi

BIBL.: Compardon 1863; Hans, Kobe-Tokyo, 2002, no. 87

The "Affair of the Diamond Necklace" was one of the biggest scandals of the last years of the reign of Louis XVI. The jewelers Boehmer and Bassenge had assembled 540 diamonds for a sumptuous necklace that no European sovereign wanted to buy because of its exorbitant price: 1.8 million *livres* (fig. 33). Louis XVI offered this huge piece of jewelry to Marie-Antoinette twice, in 1778 and 1784, and she declined both times. The comtesse de la Motte made the Prince de Rohan believe that Marie-Antoinette wanted this necklace and had asked him to buy it for her. The prince, who was also a cardinal and grand almoner of France, one of the highest dignitaries in the land, wanted to curry favor with the queen. He therefore bought the jewel in the name of the queen on January 26, 1785. A fake contract with the jewelers was transmitted to him with a forged signature of the queen. The necklace was delivered to the court but never reached the queen because Madame de la Motte and her accomplices had successfully stolen it, and then resold the diamonds in England. When the swindle was discovered, the king ordered the cardinal arrested in August 1785. In the ensuing court case, Rohan was declared innocent by the Parliament of Paris, and somehow blame was attached instead to the queen. Her enemies spread her reputation for being frivolous and spendthrift, an image that was embraced by the public and considerably weakened the position of the monarchy.

Pierre-Xavier Hans

Fig. 33 The so-called Queen's Necklace, ca. 1785. Engraving. Musée du Château de Versailles

Revolution, Imprisonment, and Execution

Fin tragique de Marie Antoinette d'Autriche Reine de France, exécutée le 16 Octobre 1793.

Condemned to death on October 16, 1793, Marie-Antoinette wrote her last words to her sister-in-law, Madame Elisabeth, "It is to you, my sister, that I write for the last time. I have just been condemned to death, not a shameful death, which is for criminals, but to rejoin your brother [Louis XVI had been executed some months earlier]. I am calm as one is when one's conscience is clear. But I deeply regret leaving my poor children."

The French Revolution was brought on by social unrest resulting from an antiquated political system, the king's inability to reform the monarchy, and a dire economic situation. The state was bankrupt, partly due to the huge costs of French involvement in the American Revolutionary War. There was also a succession of bad harvests, which caused widespread starvation among the poor. Louis XVI and Marie-Antoinette were ill equipped to deal with the fast-moving drama that fell on them after the storming of the Bastille in July 1789. Poor advice from their ministers and a lack of firmness on the king's part led to the family's capture. In October 1789 they were taken to Paris by a mob, after which they became virtual prisoners under house arrest.

After their attempt to escape failed at Varennes in 1791, the situation worsened for the royal family. Following the terrible events of the Terror of September 1792, the monarchy was abolished. The members of the royal family were locked up in the tower of the ancient, dank Temple fortress. Seen as a traitor, the king was guillotined in January 1793. The queen met the same fate in October 1793 (figs. 34, 35; cat. 19), leaving her surviving children in the care of her sister-in-law, who would also go to the guillotine. The royal family in exile declared Marie-Antoinette's son Louis XVII, but he died in prison in 1795. Only her daughter, Madame Royale, later the duchesse d'Angoûleme (1778–1851), survived the Revolution, a scarred and bitter person.

PRISE DE LA BASTILLE ,
le 14 Juillet 1789.

PIERRE-GABRIEL BERTHAULT (1748–1819)

CAT. 18 *Prise de la Bastille le 14 juillet 1789 (The Storming of the Bastille, July 14, 1789), no. 16 from the series Tableaux de la Révolution française, ca. 1800*

Engraving; 11⅜ × 11³⁄₁₆ in. (28.8 × 28.4 cm) (image); Fine Arts Museums of San Francisco, Achenbach Foundation for Graphic Arts, 1963.30.3299

PROVENANCE: Moore S. Achenbach, gift to the Achenbach Foundation for Graphic Arts, San Francisco, 1963

Regarded as the opening salvo of the French Revolution, the storming of the Bastille liberated only seven prisoners but yielded ammunition for the Parisian militia.

The Unfortunate MARIE ANTOINETTE QUEEN of FRANCE at the PLACE of EXECUTION, October 16.th 1793

This Beautiful Princess was conveyed from the Prison of the Conciergerie to the Place de la Revolution, where Louis her late Husband had suffered, amidst the whole armed Force of Paris; she still preserved her natural Dignity of Mind, and Ascended the Scaffold with seeming composure, looking Firmly around on all sides, and when she beheld the fatal Instrument her Countenance was a little changed, but soon return'd to its former serenity. The common Executioner immediately tyed her to the Board, and the Groove being fitted to her Neck, the Axe was let down and in an instant separated the Head from the Body; Thus died in the 38 Year of her Age, the Daughter of an Emperor, the Wife of a King, & the Mother of a Prince called the Dauphine at his Birth.

Published Dec.r 12 .d 1793 by John Fairburn, Map, Chart & Printseller, N.o 146 Minories, London.   (Plan II)

ANONYMOUS, BRITISH

CAT. 19 *The Unfortunate Marie Antoinette Queen of France at the Place of Execution, October 16th, 1793*, n.d.

Mezzotint; 13¾ × 9⅝ in. (35 × 24.5 cm) (image); Fine Arts Museums of San Francisco, Achenbach Foundation for Graphic Arts, 1963.30.31654

PROVENANCE: Moore S. Achenbach, gift to the Achenbach Foundation for Graphic Arts, San Francisco, 1963

The inscription on this print reads: *The Beautiful Princess was conveyed from the Prison of the Conciergerie to the Place de la Revolution, where Louis her late Husband had suffered amidst the whole armed Force of Paris; she still preserved her natural Dignity of Mind, and Ascended the Scaffold with seeming composure, looking Firmly around on all sides, and when she beheld the fatal Instrument her Countenance was a little changed, but soon return'd to its former serenity. The common Executioner immediately tyed her to the Board, and the Groove being fitted to her Neck, the Axe was let down and in an instant seperated the Head from the Body; Thus died in the 38 Year of her Age, the Daughter of an Emperor, the Wife of a King, & the Mother of a Prince called The Dauphine [sic] at his Birth.*

Published Decr. 12th, 1793 by John Fairburn, Map, Chart & Printseller no 146 Minories, London

Revival: The Cult of Marie-Antoinette

Fig. 36 Francesco Bartolozzi (ca. 1725–1815), *The Apotheosis of the French Royal Family*, 1799. Etching and engraving. Fine Arts Museums of San Francisco, gift of Archer M. Huntington, 1927.102

In this print the dead members of the French royal family are shown in the clouds above Paris, with the last victim, the young Louis XVII, being escorted by an angel.

Fig. 37 Franz Xaver Winterhalter (1805–1873), *The Empress Eugénie (Eugénie de Montijo, 1826–1920, Condesa de Teba)*, 1854. Oil on canvas. Metropolitan Museum of Art, New York. Purchase, Mr. and Mrs. Claus von Bülow Gift, 1978

The empress is depicted in eighteenth-century–style dress in emulation of Marie-Antoinette.

Marie-Antoinette and the whole royal family were portrayed in monarchic Europe as martyrs. In France, however, Marie-Antoinette's reputation recovered only when the Bourbons were restored to the throne in 1814–1815, after the failure of Napoleon's wars. With the burgeoning romanticism of the mid-nineteenth century, Marie-Antoinette was recast as the tragic martyr queen (fig. 36). Her admiring biography by the Goncourt brothers, published in 1858, inspired a new generation of followers. Empress Eugénie, wife of Napoleon III, had a fascination with Marie-Antoinette bordering on obsession. In emulation of the late queen she had herself painted by Winterhalter in eighteenth-century dress (fig. 37) and also had her great crown jewels cast in a late-eighteenth-century style (cat. 20). At her Château de Saint-Cloud the empress gathered the royal furniture associated with Marie-Antoinette that had survived the Revolution (fig. 38). In 1867 an exhibition about Marie-Antoinette was held at the Petit Trianon under the aegis of Empress Eugénie, bringing the château back to life as a testament to both the queen and the exquisitely made objects of the years preceding the Revolution. Since then the Petit Trianon has been restored as the private domain of Marie-Antoinette.

Fig. 38 Jean-Baptiste Fortuné de Fournier (1798–1864), *The Cabinet de Toilette of the Empress Eugénie at the Château de Saint-Cloud*, ca. 1860. Compiègne, musée national du château

In the 1850s and 1860s the empress furnished her rooms with pieces thought to have belonged to Marie-Antoinette.

CAT. 20   Bow and tassel brooch,
ca. 1855

KRAMER, PARIS

Diamonds set in silver; 8⅜ × 4⅛ in. (22 × 10.5 cm);
Private collection, New York

PROVENANCE: The French crown jewels; Empress Eugénie; sale of the French crown jewels, Paris, May 12–23,
1887, lot 5; Astor Family, New York; Private collection,
New York

BIBL.: Morel 1988, pp. 340, 367, 376–377

Created for Empress Eugénie, this jewel was originally part of a large belt made by the Parisian jeweler Kramer in about 1855. The belt was remodeled in 1864, but the central portion, seen here, was reserved as a great brooch. It is one of several jewels made for the empress in the style of the late eighteenth century.

Designed as a flamboyantly naturalistic bow with two weighty tassels, the jewel is hung with an unmistakably mid-nineteenth-century feature, the five pendants of large diamonds known as *pampilles*. Composed of 2,438 brilliant-cut diamonds and 196 small rose-cut diamonds, this piece was made from the diamonds of the French crown jewels, some of which had managed to survive through the depredations of the Revolution to this point in 1850s. Some of the diamonds used in this brooch may indeed have formed part of the jewels worn by Marie-Antoinette, which were stolen during the Revolution in a massive and extended theft from September 11 to 17, 1792. What was recovered was used to finance the Revolutionary campaigns by the Directory and Consulate. When Napoleon took power he retrieved what he could and created a rich treasury of diamonds. The French crown jewels underwent a last great transformation under Napoleon III for the Empress Eugénie, whose beauty, fashion sense, and ability to wear large amounts of jewelry were the best advertisement the jewelers of Paris could ask for. After the fall of the Second Empire the crown jewels were put in storage. They were exhibited only twice, in 1878 at the Paris Exposition and again in 1884, before nearly all were sold by the Third Republic in a huge sale in 1887. The brooch is kept in its original box stamped *Diamants de la Couronne de France.*

Martin Chapman

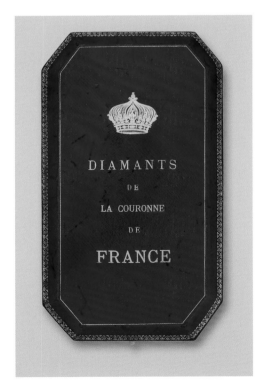

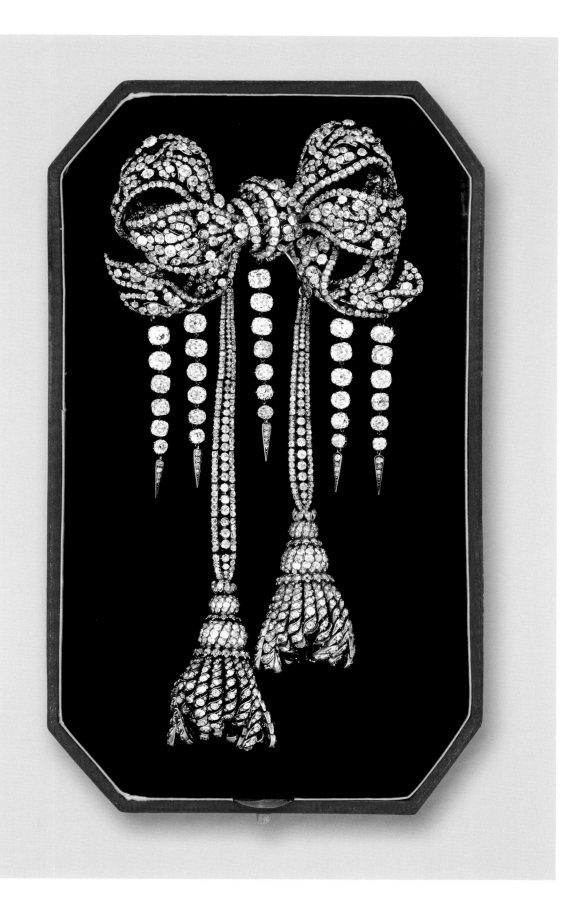

PETIT TRIANON

View of the Petit Trianon, ca. 1867, from Lescure's *Les Palais de Trianon*. Wood engraving

Page 94.

MATHURIN DE LESCURE (1833–1892)

CAT. 21 *Les Palais de Trianon, Histoire—
Description. Catalogue des objects
exposés sous les auspices de sa Majesté
l'Imperatrice,* Paris, n.d. [1867]

Private collection

Under the auspices of Empress Eugénie, in 1867 an exhibition about Marie-Antoinette was held at the Petit Trianon. The accompanying book gives a full account of the history of the Petit Trianon and includes a catalogue of the exhibition. Several objects, such as the famous gilt-bronze lantern (cat. 41), listed as no. 1 in the catalogue, are still today in the collection of the Petit Trianon.

Martin Chapman

Fig. 39 The entrance facade of the Petit Trianon. Water-
color by Claude-Louis Châtelet (1750–1795), in *Souvenir
Album of the Petit Trianon,* 1781 (cat. 63). Private collection,
New York

II The Petit Trianon and Marie-Antoinette

Built originally as a *maison de plaisance* (pleasure house) for King Louis XV, the Petit Trianon was given to Marie-Antoinette by Louis XVI after their accession in 1774 (fig. 39). The king made Marie-Antoinette mistress of her own domain by presenting her with a special key decorated with 531 diamonds. Thereafter, everything was done *par ordre de la reine* (on the queen's orders), and no one visited without her permission. The tiny château, secluded in a distant corner of the park at Versailles, was the queen's retreat from court life. Here, the queen said, "je suis moi" (I am myself). The Petit Trianon afforded Marie-Antoinette and her friends a measure of privacy and a place to relax. The intimates of the queen's inner circle spent their time reading, doing needlework, playing cards, making music, or singing. In contrast to the formal etiquette at the court of Versailles, there was little royal protocol, and instead of leaping to their feet each time the queen entered the room, guests would continue with their activities.

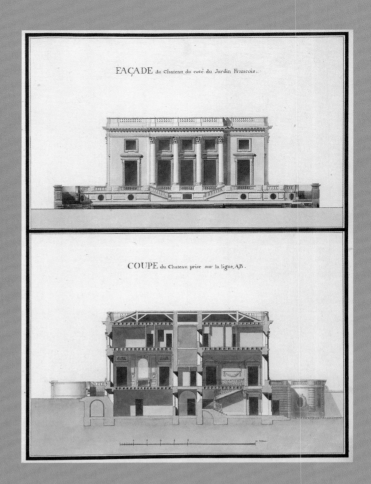

FAÇADE du Chateau du coté du Jardin François.

COUPE du Chateau prise sur la ligne AB.

Early History of the Château and Gardens

Fig. 40 The Petit Trianon from the French gardens. Pen-and-ink drawings (elevation and section) by Richard Mique (1728–1794), in *Souvenir Album of the Petit Trianon*, 1781 (cat. 63). Private collection, New York

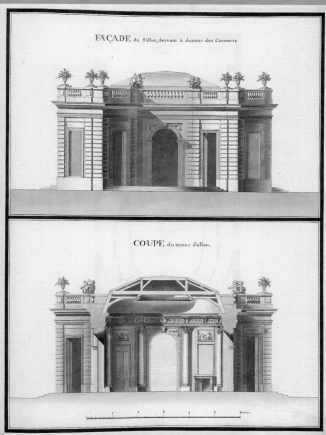

L ouis XV built the Petit Trianon in his botanical gardens at Versailles in 1762–1768. It was a project of his famous mistress Madame de Pompadour, but she died before it was completed. Her successor, Madame Du Barry, was its first female occupant. The château was intended as a retreat from the court, a place where the king could live a simple life. The court architect Ange-Jacques Gabriel gave Louis XV an architectural icon that is regarded as one of the most perfect examples of French neoclassical design (fig. 40). The almost severe, boxlike form is discreetly relieved with delicate, classical ornament of the Corinthian order. The balanced proportions of the facades and the elegant restraint ushered in the new style of neoclassical architecture.

The interior of the château was outfitted with relatively simple decoration, much of it with a floral theme. The paneling, carved by Honoré Guibert in 1765, had a scheme of fruit and flowers. Guibert also carved the stonework on the great staircase, and François Brochois made the iron balustrade of the stairs, which bears the monogram of *MA* for Marie-Antoinette (fig. 41).

Louis XV constructed extensive botanical gardens at the Petit Trianon, as well as a dairy and a menagerie for domestic, rather than exotic, animals. The gardens were divided into sections for flowers and vegetables and boasted more than 4,000 different plants. The king's architect designed two pavilions: the French Pavilion (fig. 42), built in 1750 at the center of the garden, and the Pavillon Frais ("cool" pavilion), which was used for dining.

Fig. 41 Detail of the stair railing by François Brochois in the main hall of the Petit Trianon. The monogram of *MA* is for Marie-Antoinette.

Fig. 42 The French Pavilion in the gardens of the Petit Trianon. Pen-and-ink drawings (elevation and section) by Richard Mique (1728–1794), in *Souvenir Album of the Petit Trianon*, 1781 (cat. 63). Private collection, New York

François-Hubert Drouais (1727–1775)

CAT. 22 *Louis XV at Sixty-Three Years of Age,* 1773

Signed and dated lower left: *Drouais / en aoust / 1773*; Oil on canvas; 28½ × 23⅜ in. (72.5 × 59.5 cm); Inv. MV 4438

PROVENANCE: Painted without official commission in 1773 and shown at the Paris Salon of that year (no. 77); entered Versailles during the reign of Louis-Philippe

BIBL.: Engerand 1900, p. 169; Gabillot 1906, p. 170; Salmon 2007, pp. 114–117 and 217–218, no. 36, repr.

We have few portraits of Louis XV after 1765 because the king did not enjoy granting sittings. Artists often had to be satisfied with working from earlier images of the monarch's face. Therefore, this portrait by Drouais, painted in 1773 shortly before the king's death, is quite exceptional. It is one of the last two portraits of Louis XV, the other being the one executed that same year by Armand-Vincent de Montpetit (1713–1800), a copy of which is at Versailles (Inv. MV 8452).

When the painting was exhibited at the Salon of 1773, the critic Pidansat de Mayrobert wrote: "[The painter] has absolutely failed in the too-youthful portrait of the King, whose eyes he has narrowed and to whom he has shown disrespect with an attitude that is less than *spirituelle.*" If the work did not please, it is probably because Drouais applied to a royal person a composition normally employed for commoners.

Xavier Salmon

CARLE VANLOO (1705–1765)

CAT. 23 *Madame de Pompadour as a Gardener*, 1754–1755

Inscribed on the back: *Carle Vanloo*; Oil on canvas; 32 × 25⅜ in. (81.2 × 64.5 cm); Inv. MV 8616

PROVENANCE: Sale of the marquis de Ménars, the marquise's brother, Paris, March 18–April 6, 1782, lot 130; sold to François Basan; Abraham Fontanel (1750–1813) Collection, Montpellier; Paulme Collection in 1903; J. Pierpont Morgan Collection, London, in 1907; Knoedler Galleries, New York, in 1943; Purchased by Mrs. W. J. MacCormick in 1945; sale, Sotheby's, London, April 19, 1967, lot 27; Mrs. Hudson Vandergrift Collection; Didier Aaron Ltd., London; purchased by the Château de Versailles in 1992

BIBL.: Wine 2002, pp. 158–160, no. 34, repr.

AFTER AUGUSTIN PAJOU (1730–1809)

CAT. 24 *Madame Du Barry,* 1850–1900

Signed lower back: *PAJOU*;
Marble; 22¾ × 18½ × 11 in.
(57.5 × 47 × 28 cm); Fine
Arts Museums of San
Francisco, gift of André J.
Kahn-Wolf, 1962.8

PROVENANCE: André J. Kahn-Wolf, Paris, by whom given
to the California Palace of the Legion of Honor, 1962

BIBL.: *Madame Du Barry* 1992, p. 126; Draper and Scherf
1997, pp. 237–246, no. 97

This is a later copy of the famous portrait of Madame Du
Barry now at the Louvre.

CAT. 25 Card table

GILLES JOUBERT (1689–1775), MASTER CA. 1714

Stamped *Joubert JME*; registration mark *du Nº* of the journal of the Garde-Meuble de la Couronne; brand-mark of the Petit Trianon: crowned *CT*; round mark of the Garde-Meuble de la Couronne; Oak and cherry wood, with lines of kingwood; 28½ × 31¼ × 15¾ in. (72.5 × 79.3 × 40 cm); Inv. V 5250

PROVENANCE: Delivered for Louis XV to the Petit Trianon in 1768; purchased in 1985

BIBL.: Arizzoli-Clémentel 2002, pp. 135–136, no. 45

This table is the only piece of furniture known to have come from Louis XV's Petit Trianon.

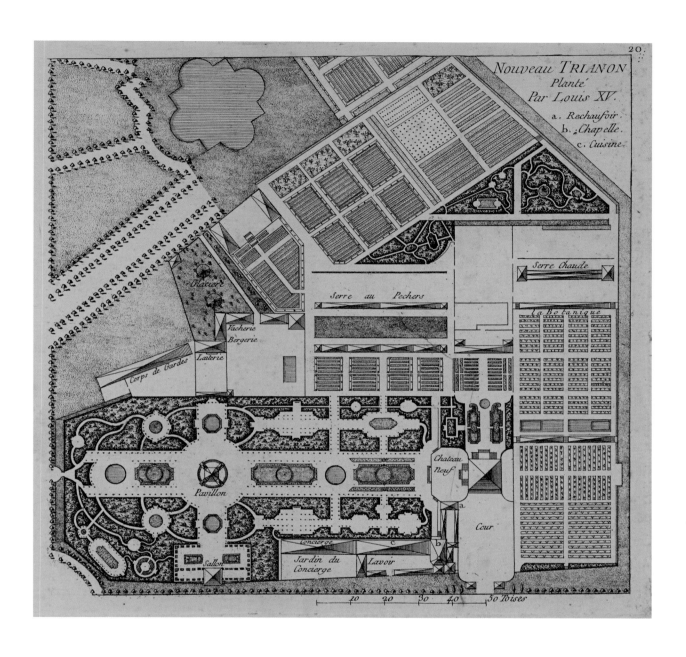

The following labels appear within the plan:

Nouveau TRIANON
Planté
Par Louis XV.

a. *Rechaufoir.*
b. *Chapelle.*
c. *Cuisine.*

Glaciere

Serre Chaude

Serre au Pechers

La Botanique

Vacherie
Bergerie
Laiterie
Corps de Gardes

Chateau
Neuf

a

Cour

Pavillon

b

c

Sallon

Concierge

Jardin du
Concierge

Lavoir

10   20   30   40   50 Toises

FRENCH SCHOOL, SECOND HALF OF THE 18TH CENTURY

CAT. 26   *The New Trianon, Planted by Louis XV*

Engraving and etching on
cream-colored paper; 9⅝ ×
10 in. (24.5 × 25.5 cm); Inv.
grav. 640

PROVENANCE: Old collection of the Château de
Versailles

JACQUES-ANDRÉ PORTAIL (1695–1759)

CAT. 27 *Panoramic View of the Trianon Gardens,* n.d.

Graphite with watercolor highlights on oiled paper; 9 × 6½ in. (23 × 16.5 cm); Inv. MV 6162, Inv. dessins 647

PROVENANCE: Gabrielli Collection, Paris; Gabrielli estate sale, Hôtel Drouot, Paris, March 19, 1934; purchased by David David-Weill as a gift to the Château de Versailles in April 1934

BIBL.: Salmon 2001, p. 51, no. 22, repr.

François-Denis Née (1732–1817), after Louis-Nicolas de Lespinasse (1734–1808)

CAT. 28 *The Pavillon Français in the French Garden of the Petit Trianon. Fourth View of the Château de Trianon in the French Garden,* n.d.

Etching; 7¼ × 9⅝ in. (18.3 × 24.5 cm); Inv. gravures 501

PROVENANCE: Old Collections of the Château de Versailles

The Antechamber and Dining Room

Fig. 43 The antechamber at the Petit Trianon

Fig. 44 The dining room at the Petit Trianon

The antechamber is the first room the visitor enters on the main floor of the Petit Trianon (fig. 43). In 1777 Marie-Antoinette ordered two marble busts from the sculptor Louis-Simon Boizot, one of Louis XVI and the other of her brother Emperor Joseph II of Austria. Memorializing the two most important men in the queen's life, the busts were placed in the antechamber that same year, after Joseph II's visit to Versailles.

The dining room is today still largely as it was designed for Louis XV in the 1760s (fig. 44). Honoré Guibert carved the paneling with appropriate emblems of the feast: fruit and flowers. In the grand tradition of French history painting, the room's four paintings are allegories of subjects related to dining: fishing, the harvest, hunting, and the wine harvest. The extensive nudity in the painting of fishing was not to Marie-Antoinette's taste, and she requested replacements. She asked her mother, the empress Maria-Theresa, to send copies of her favorite paintings from her youth in Vienna, one of which portrays the queen as a young archduchess dancing at the celebration for her brother's marriage in 1765 (cats. 1, 2). None of the room's original furnishings have survived.

LOUIS-SIMON BOIZOT (1743–1809)

CAT. 29 *Louis XVI, King of France (1754–1793), 1777*

Marble; 30¾ × 20½ × 14⅛ in. (78 × 52 × 36 cm); Signed on the back: *par Boizot 1777*; Inv. MR 2134 (MV 5789)

PROVENANCE: Commissioned by Marie-Antoinette; shown at the 1777 Salon (no. 257); placed in the anteroom of the Petit Trianon in 1777; transferred to the Château de Saint-Cloud in 1827; reinstalled in its original location in 1831

BIBL.: Hoog 1993, p. 246; Piquenard 1999, pp. 484–485

EXH.: Versailles, 1955, no. 122; Versailles, 2001–2002, no. 12

The king, in court dress, wears the order of the Golden Fleece and the ribbon of the order of the Holy Spirit; the badge of the order is also pinned on his jacket. Despite these attributes, however, the bust does not present a formal, royal image, especially compared with Augustin Pajou's official portrait bust (known by a 1779 version, Musée national des Châteaux de Versailles et de Trianon, Inv. MR 2652–MV 7097). Instead Boizot portrayed the king with a more casual demeanor. Although the king carries his head in a rather haughty manner, he has a good-natured expression on his face, with the hint of a smile.

A skilled portraitist, Boizot did not depict some of his royal sitter's more unfortunate features, notably, his oval face, which the artist deliberately made thinner than it appears in other contemporary painted and sculpted likenesses of Louis XVI (cat. 52). He thereby gave the head "a certain refinement that, in the opinion of those courtiers who had had the honor of being in the presence of the monarch, was not the most distinctive feature of his appearance" (Pidansat de Mairobert, *Mémoires secrets pour servir à l'histoire de la République des Lettres en France*).

Conceived as a pendant to the bust of Joseph II (cat. 30), Marie-Antoinette's brother and the emperor of Austria, the informal bust of Louis XVI was appropriate for its intended location at the Trianon—a retreat reserved for the queen, a place where the rigid court protocol had no part. The two busts were commissioned on the occasion of the emperor's visit to France and perpetuated the memory of a particularly happy visit.

Alexandre Maral

LOUIS-SIMON BOIZOT (1743–1809)

CAT. 30 *Joseph II, Emperor of Austria (1741–1790)*, 1777

Marble; 31⅞ × 22 × 14⅛ in. (81 × 56 × 36 cm); Signed on the back: *Joseph II empereur fait à Paris en 1777 d'après nature par Boizot* [Joseph II emperor made in Paris in 1777 from life by Boizot]; Inv. MR 2132 (MV 2150)

PROVENANCE: Commissioned by Marie-Antoinette; shown at the 1777 Salon (no. 258); placed in the anteroom of the Petit Trianon in 1777; transferred to the Château de Saint-Cloud in 1827; reinstalled in its original location in 1831

BIBL.: Hoog 1993, p. 203; Piquenard 1999, pp. 484–485

EXH.: Versailles, 1955, no. 178; Paris, 1958, no. 122; Versailles, 2001–2002, no. 13

When Joseph II, Marie-Antoinette's brother, visited France from April to July 1777, he went under the pseudonym of the comte de Falkenstein. The simplicity of his manners and lifestyle surprised both the Parisians and the court at Versailles. During his stay, Marie-Antoinette had this bust made for the recently redecorated Petit Trianon. She was very fond of her brother, who would play a discreet but vital role as marriage counselor.

The bust, commissioned together with one of Louis XVI (cat. 29), displays remarkable skill and psychological insight. Boizot contrasted the sober, yet subtle, rendering of the face with the luxurious drape of the cloak around the shoulders. Thérese Picquenard wrote: "The taste for contrast and the drapery technique are unmistakable signs of Slodtz's influence upon his student."

The angles of the faces, the sober hairstyles, and the iteration of the insignia of the orders of the Golden Fleece and the Holy Spirit suggest that the two busts were conceived as pendants. The emperor wears a breastplate while the king is in court dress, but both wear a similar cloak. This prestigious commission is particularly well documented in the archives: the young Boizot—who had been director of the sculpture studio of the Royal Porcelain Manufactory at Sèvres since 1773—was paid the handsome sum of eight thousand *livres* for the busts and their stands. This mark of the queen's confidence in an artist who was as yet neither established nor publicly recognized is somewhat surprising, although Boizot had already sculpted a much-admired bust of Marie-Antoinette that was shown at the Salon of 1775. Furthermore, during his 1777 stay, Joseph II made an extended visit to the workshops of the Sèvres factory, where he would have had ample opportunity to meet the sculptor. In any event, Boizot worked from life, as the inscription on the back of the bust attests. In addition to presenting the two busts at the 1777 Salon, the sculptor shrewdly garnered publicity for his works by marketing them in the form of small Sèvres biscuitware reproductions (cat. 6). This royal commission moved Boizot to the forefront of the art scene, allowing him to become a career sculptor specializing in portraiture. The two Trianon busts are incontrovertible evidence of a pivotal moment in his career.

Alexandre Maral

GABRIEL-FRANÇOIS DOYEN (1726–1806)

CAT. 31 *La pêche (Fishing)*, n.d.

Oil on canvas; 9 ft. 1 in. × 8 ft. 3⅜ in. (2.77 × 2.53 m);
Inv. MV 6189

LOUIS LAGRENÉE THE ELDER (1725–1805)

CAT. 32 *La moisson, ou Cèrès et
Triptolème (The Harvest, or Ceres and
Triptolemus)*, 1769

Signed and dated lower left: *Louis Lagrenée 1769*; Oil
on canvas; 10 ft. 9½ in. × 7 ft. 4¼ in. (3.29 × 2.24 m);
Inv. MV 7416

JOSEPH-MARIE VIEN (1716–1809)

CAT. 33 *La chasse (The Hunt)*, 1772

Signed and dated lower right: *Jo. M. Vien 1772*; Oil on canvas; 10 ft. 9½ in. × 7 ft. 7 in. (3.29 × 2.31 m); Inv. MV 7415

NOËL HALLÉ (1711–1781)

CAT. 34 *La vendange, ou le Triomphe de
Bacchus (The Grape Harvest, or the
Triumph of Bacchus)*, 1776

Signed and dated lower right: *Hallé 1776*; 9 ft. 1 in. × 8 ft.
4⅜ in. (2.77 × 2.55 m); Inv. 6193

PROVENANCE: Commissioned for the dining room of the
Petit Trianon in 1768; *La moisson (The Harvest)* shown at
the Salon of 1769, *La chassse (The Hunt)* at the Salon of
1773; all in situ until the Revolution, except for *La pêche
(Fishing)*, which was deemed too indecorous and removed
in 1774 (replaced with another version of *La vendange [The
Grape Harvest]*, painted by Jean-Baptiste Marie Pierre); all
four mentioned as being in the Musée central des Arts in
Paris in 1794; dispersed to the Beauvais tapestry manufactory and the châteaux of Fontainebleau and Compiègne;
restored to their places at the Petit Trianon in the twentieth century

A group of four paintings was commissioned in 1768 for the large dining room at the Petit Trianon. The subjects, determined by Charles-Nicolas Cochin, secretary of the Académie Royale de Pein-ture, in February 1768, were allegorical celebrations of food and drink. After some hesitation about the choice of artists—since Jean-Baptiste-Marie Pierre, first painter to the king, had already executed a canvas representing the grape harvest—Doyen was assigned *La pêche (Fishing)*, which depicts Neptune and Amphitrite surrounded by nymphs and tritons; Vien *La chasse (The Hunt)*, which shows Diana sharing her game with nymphs and peasants; Lagrenée the Elder *La moisson (The Harvest)*, in which Ceres and Triptolemus dis-tribute grain and teach people the art of preparing wheat; and Hallé *La vendange (The Grape Harvest)*, which portrays Bacchus and peas-ants harvesting grapes.

Vien's and Lagrenée's paintings were well received, but Doyen and Hallé's were not. Hallé's composition was replaced with Pierre's painting on the same subject (Château de Versailles). As early as 1774 Marie-Antoinette had apparently indicated that she disliked Doyen's painting because it displayed female figures considered unseemly. She had asked to have it removed from the dining room and replaced with another composition. Invited to submit another painting, Doyen at first attempted to change the existing composition but then abandoned the project. On July 14, 1776, Pierre suggested to the comte d'Angiviller, *surintendant des bâtiments*, that Doyen's *La pêche (Fishing)* be substituted with Hallé's *La vendange (The Grape Harvest)*, that is, the work that had displeased the queen and that had been replaced earlier. On July 22, D'Angiviller agreed. If the queen still maintained her poor opinion of Hallé's painting, he would order another one to take its place.

Pierre's proposed solution failed to satisfy Marie-Antoinette. In 1778, she asked her mother to obtain Johann Georg Weikert's copies of two works in Vienna (cats. 1, 2). However, it is not known whether Weikert's two replicas were hung in the dining room. If they were, it was only temporarily, because their placement with Vien's *La chasse (The Hunt)* and Lagrenée's *La moisson (The Harvest)* certainly frac-tured Cochin's handsome iconographic program. In 1792, Weikert's paintings were both in the Grand Trianon. The official report on the paintings taken from the Petit Trianon on 13 April 1794 reveals that the paintings by Vien, Hallé, Pierre, and Lagrenée had adorned the dining room until then.

Xavier Salmon

CAT. 31 DOYEN *La pêche (Fishing)*

CAT. 32 LAGRENÉE THE ELDER *La moisson, ou Cérès et Triptolème (The Harvest, or Ceres and Triptolemus)*

CAT. 34 HALLÉ *La vendange, ou le Triomphe de Bacchus (The Grape Harvest, or the Triumph of Bacchus)*

CAT. 35 Plate from the "Pearl and
Cornflower" service of Marie-
Antoinette, 1781

Royal Porcelain Manufactory, Sèvres; Mark of the painter
Choisy; mark of the gilder Michel-Barnabé Chauveaux
the Elder; Soft-paste porcelain; 1³⁄₁₆ × diam. 9⁷⁄₁₆ in. (3 ×
24 cm); v5365

PROVENANCE: Given by Charles Otto Zieseniss, 1991

BIBL.: Baulez 1991, pp. 62–76, repr. p. 70, fig. 11; Hans,
Bordeaux, 2005, p. 152, no. 55a

CAT. 36 Salad bowl from the "Pearl
and Cornflower" service of Marie-
Antoinette, 1781

Royal Porcelain Manufactory, Sèvres; Marked *L.B.* for the
painter Jean-Nicolas Lebel; mark of the gilder Louis-Francois
Lécot; Soft-paste porcelain; 3¾ × diam. 9¹⁄₁₆ in. (8.2 ×
23 cm); v 5856

PROVENANCE: Acquired by the Château de Versailles in
1998, gift of the Société des Amis de Versailles

BIBL.: Baulez 1998, p. 92

During the summer of 1781 the queen ordered a new porcelain dinner service from the royal Sèvres factory. Designed with strings of pearls encircling a border of scattered cornflowers, the "Pearl and Cornflower" service comprised some 295 pieces. Another, simpler service was probably made for the receptions to welcome distinguished foreign guests to the Petit Trianon. The design certainly reflected the "rustic" character of the Petit Trianon. The queen loved cornflowers, which are also found on another one of her porcelain services (cat. 13). The pattern also proved popular with both the queen's sisters-in-law, the comtesses de Provence and d'Artois, both of whom had variants made for them at Sèvres.

Pierre-Xavier Hans

CAT. 37 Plate from the "Pearl and Cornflower" service of
the comtesse de Provence, 1781

Royal Porcelain Manufac-
tory, Sèvres; Marked *LL*
with date-letters *dd* for
1781; mark of the painter
Michel-Gabriel Commelin;
mark of the gilder Michel-
Barnabé Chauveaux the
Elder; Hard-paste porce-
lain; 1 × diam. 9 in. (2.7 ×
23 cm); Inv. v5763

PROVENANCE: Purchased in 1995

BIBL.: Baulez 1996, p. 94; Hans, Bordeaux, 2005, p. 153,
no. 56a

CAT. 38 Plate from the "Pearl and Cornflower" service of the comtesse d'Artois, 1788

Royal Porcelain Manufactory, Sèvres; Marked *LL* with date-letters *ll* for 1788; mark of the painter Marie-Anne Vautrin; Hard-paste porcelain; 1 × diam. 9½ in. (2.7 × 24 cm); Inv. v5764

PROVENANCE: Purchased in 1995

BIBL.: Baulez 1996, p. 94; Hans, Bordeaux, 2005, p. 153, no. 56b

The *Salon de compagnie*

Fig. 45 The *salon de compagnie* at the Petit Trianon

In the *salon de compagnie,* or drawing room, the queen entertained her guests, who pursued their own amusements: reading, playing games, and making music (fig. 45). Her favorite members of the inner circle included the duchesse de Polignac (fig. 46) and her sister-in-law Madame Elisabeth (cat. 39). This salon remains largely as it was in Louis XV's time. Guibert's carved paneling, with its large-scale carving of lilies, interlaced Ls, and crowns of roses, is part of the room's original decoration (fig. 18). The upholstered chairs resemble the original furniture supplied for the room, which was also painted white. They are covered in the same fabric that was used there in the 1770s. The most famous object in the room is the lantern attributed to the bronzeworker Pierre-Philippe Thomire. The Petit Trianon was a summer house, and, as windows were often left open, lanterns were necessary to prevent the candles from being extinguished accidentally. This sumptuous lantern, made of expensive gilt bronze and decorated with blue enamel varnish and imitation gemstones, has become the icon of the château and has been much copied.

Fig. 46 Elisabeth Louise Vigée Le Brun (1755–1842), *Gabrielle Yolande Claude Martine de Polastron, duchesse de Polignac (1749–1793),* 1782. Oil on canvas. Musée du Château de Versailles

Marie-Antoinette's closest friend in the 1780s, the duchesse de Polignac was the most beautiful member of the queen's inner circle. She spent much time at the Petit Trianon.

ELISABETH LOUISE VIGÉE LE BRUN (1755–1842)

CAT. 39 *Madame Elisabeth, Sister of Louis XVI,* n.d.

Oil on canvas; 43¼ × 32¼ in. (1.10 m × 82 cm); Inv. MV8143

PROVENANCE: Comte des Cars Collection; gift in 1961 to the Château de Versailles from the marquise d'Oncieu de Chaffardon and her sister Mlle. Beatrix de Bertier de Sauvigny, granddaughters of the comte des Cars

BIBL.: Vigée Le Brun 1835–1837, vol. 1, p. 331; Salmon, Bordeaux, 2005, pp. 106–107, no. 27, repr.

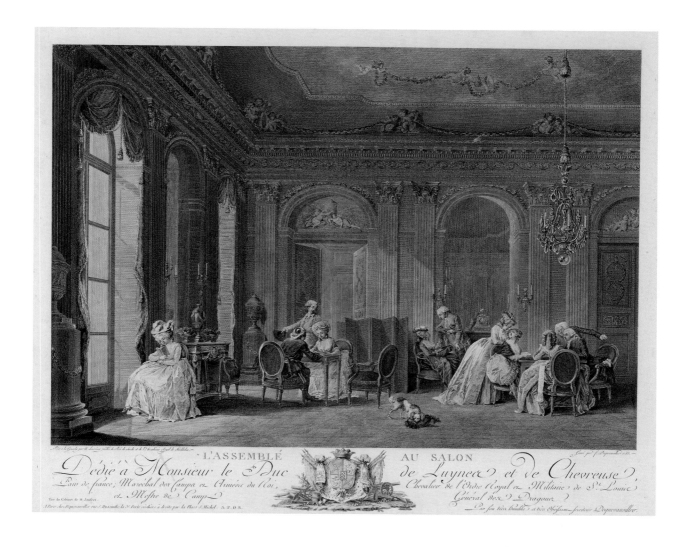

L'ASSEMBLÉ AU SALON

Dédié à Monsieur le Duc de Luynes et de Chevreuse,

NICHOLAS-BARTHELÉMY FRANÇOIS DEQUEVAUVILLIER (1745–1807)

AFTER NICOLAS LAVREINCE (NIKLAS LAFRENSEN) (SWEDEN, 1737–1807)

CAT. 40 *L'Assemblé au salon (Gathering in a Salon)*, ca. 1780

Line engraving; 16 × 19⅝ in. (40.5 × 50 cm) (image); 17⅞ × 21½ in. (45.3 × 54.5 cm) (sheet); Fine Arts Museums of San Francisco, museum purchase, Achenbach Foundation for Graphic Arts Endowment Fund, 1964

PROVENANCE: Bought from C. G. Boerner for the Achenbach Foundation for Graphic Arts, 1964

BIBL.: Portalis and Beraldi 1880, p. 741 (1); Lawrence–Dighton 44/IV

This interior of a fashionable French salon of the 1780s shows what life must have been like in the *salon de compagnie* at the Petit Trianon. Guests pursued their own activities of reading, playing backgammon, conversing, playing cards, and (not shown in this print) making music. The atmosphere was very informal; when the queen entered the room, members of her inner circle were expected to continue whatever they were doing without getting up.

Martin Chapman

ATTRIBUTED TO PIERRE-PHILIPPE
THOMIRE (1751–1843), MASTER IN 1772

Chased and gilt bronze, varnish (enamel), imitation gemstones; 68¼ × diam. 31½ in. (1.75 m × 80 cm); Inv. T 462

PROVENANCE: *Salon de compagnie* of the Petit Trianon, removed in 1793; 1811–1836, salon of the French Pavilion; 1836–1859, queen's staircase at the Château de Versailles; 1859–1867, the court usher's salon in the empress's apartments at the Palais des Tuileries; 1867, stairhall of the Petit Trianon; returned to the *salon de compagnie*

BIBL.: Williamson 1882/II, pl. 65; Champeaux 1882/II, p. 392; Havard IV, pl. 16; Robiquet 1912, pp. 72–73, 141–142, and 164, pl. X; Verlet 1987, pp. 376–377, fig. 384; Ledoux-Lebard 1989, p. 120; Baulez 1990, pp. 22 and 34; Baulez 1996, p. 24

EXH.: 1867, no. 1

This drum-shaped lantern is composed of four panes of glass in a gilt-bronze frame, which is partially varnished in lapis blue and decorated with imitation diamonds. The four vertical members of the frame connect the two horizontal bands, which are decorated with allegories of the four seasons. On the upper band are four musical trophies, while the lower band rests on four zephyr heads. The frame is suspended from four stretched archery bows; the bows are connected by a star-spangled band and meet at the top in a quiver of arrows. The chandelier is suspended from a flaming torch surrounded by three young, music-making fauns seated on cushions.

This lantern, included in the 1793 Revolutionary sales of the Versailles furniture, immediately became known as "the Trianon's famous lantern." It was back on the market again in 1811, when it was purchased by the imperial Garde-Meuble. It was returned to the Trianon, where it was placed in the round salon of the French Pavilion. In 1836 Louis-Philippe had it hung in the queen's staircase at the Château de Versailles, and in 1859 Empress Eugénie claimed it for the court usher's salon in her apartments at the Tuileries. The lantern returned to the Trianon in 1867 on the occasion of the exhibition the empress dedicated to the memory of Marie-Antoinette, whom she greatly admired. At that time the lantern was placed over the château's stairway, where it remained until it was recently returned to the *salon de compagnie*, for which it was created two centuries earlier.

As the fashion for lanterns developed over the course of the eighteenth century, their decoration attained an unprecedented degree of luxury. Once reserved for stairways and anterooms, where their glazed frames sheltered the flames from drafts, they began appearing in corner salons, which tended to have cross breezes. The Delaroue brothers made many fine lanterns for Louis XV at the Trianon— where there were many corner rooms—as well as a crystal chandelier for the central *salon de compagnie*. In 1784, Marie-Antoinette commissioned this very opulent lantern to take the place of the chandelier in the *salon de compagnie*, even though it was not a corner room.

This magnificent lantern, one of the finest of its time, was frequently copied after 1867 by great nineteenth-century bronzeworkers such as Beurdeley, Marquis, and Millet, but its creator remained unknown. In the nineteenth century, it was considered to be by Pierre Gouthière, to whom the finest bronzes of the Louis XVI period were frequently attributed. In 1910 it was inaccurately attributed to the lantern maker Lafond, who had merely resold it in 1811. It is now more plausibly attributed to Pierre-Philippe Thomire. In 1785 Gouthière, ruined and bankrupt, was no longer in a position to make such an object. And it does not appear in the archives of François Rémond, another candidate. Pierre-Charles Bonnefoy du Plan, keeper of Marie-Antoinette's private Garde-Meuble beginning in 1784, made Thomire—who styled himself *ciseleur-doreur du roi et de la reine* (chaser-gilder to the king and queen)—responsible

for "the materials and finished products made for the queen, in her apartments in the Petit Trianon." It is likely that Jean-Démosthène Dugourc designed the ornamentation, given that in his autobiography the artist boasts of having overseen "all the valuable bronzes executed for ten years for the famous Gouthière . . . as well as those executed for the queen by various artists." A design securely attributed to Dugourc shows the four eaglets that were originally on top of the bows. Mistaken for Napoleonic symbols, they were removed in 1815 and 1870, and they remain lost to this day.

Christian Baulez

CAT. 42 Writing table made for the
Petit Trianon, probably for Madame
Elisabeth, ca. 1784

JEAN-HENRI RIESENER (1734–1806),
MASTER IN 1768

Stamped *J.H.RIESENER* (traces) and brand of the queen's
Garde-Meuble, with a painted mark of the Petit Trianon;
a crowned *CT* and *du N° 35./I.*; Oak; marquetry of satinwood, sycamore, citron wood, maple, holly, and boxwood;
gilt bronze; 26¼ × 31¾ × 19 in. (66.7 × 80.6 × 48.2 cm);
Inv. v5288

PROVENANCE: Commissioned by Marie-Antoinette for
the Petit Trianon; sold in 1793; purchased by the Château
de Versailles in 1988

BIBL.: De Bellaigue 1974, vol. 2, no. 103; Parker 1979,
p. 114; Baulez 1990, pp. 104–105; Arizzoli-Clémentel
2002, pp. 150–151

This small piece belongs to a fairly limited group of similarly shaped writing tables made for the royal family from 1777 to 1785 by Jean-Henri Riesener, the official cabinetmaker of the Garde-Meuble. The tables display a subtle gradation of decorative opulence in relation to the importance of the person for whom the table was made. The earliest table of this design, today at Waddesdon Manor, was executed in 1777 for the king's private study at the Petit Trianon. The most richly ornamented of the group, it is decorated with marquetry alluding to Poetry and Literature, as well as chased and gilded bronzes, including a an openwork gallery running around the top edge.

Three years later, on July 10, 1780, Riesener delivered to the Petit Trianon for the queen's use "a writing table with 'mosaic' [trellis-work] marquetry; rosettes and groups of colored flowers in rosewood, inserts of white and black lines inlaid against an amaranth background; with one large drawer that locks with a key and a pull-out writing slide covered in black velvet framed with gold braid; with a side drawer fitted with inkwell, pounce pot, and sponge-box of silver-plated copper; the table decorated with moldings, capitals, rods, frames, handles, rings, and feet of bronze chased and gilded with *ormoulu* [ground gold]." In November of that year, Riesener made a piece of the same model for the queen's use at Compiègne.

The table shown here does not bear the entry number of the Garde-Meuble de la Couronne, and therefore it cannot be the one made in 1780 for the queen, despite its close resemblance. It must have been commissioned directly by the queen's private Garde-Meuble, in 1784 at the earliest, when the Garde-Meuble de la Reine was established. The marquetry bouquet of flowers on the tabletop suggests that if the table was not made for the queen it was made for a princess of the royal family, in all likelihood Madame Elisabeth, the queen's sister-in-law, who had an apartment at the Petit Trianon. Another discreet illusion to the royal family is the sunflower motif, found on the compartments of the trompe-l'oeil trelliswork.

On August 2, 1782, Riesener supplied to the duchesse de Polignac, a close friend of the queen who also lived at the château, a similar table that lacked the marquetry panel with the bouquet of flowers. The difference in the degree of ornamentation between the two tables was indicative of the status of the intended users.

Bertrand Rondot

CAT. 43 Commode, ca. 1785

JEAN-HENRI RIESENER (1734–1806), MASTER IN 1768

Stamped *J.H.RIESENER* (twice), brand-marks of the Garde-Meuble de la Reine, and the painted mark of the Château de Trianon: crowned *CT* and *Du N° 35*; Oak, with marquetry of rosewood, ebony, boxwood, and mahogany; white veined marble top; gilt bronze; 35½ × 53⅝ × 23⅜ in. (90.2 × 136.3 × 60 cm); Inv. V4945

PROVENANCE: Commissioned by the queen for the Petit Trianon; sold in 1793; purchased by the Château de Versailles in 1974

BIBL.: Meyer 1974, p. 282, fig. 4; Pradère 1989, fig. 467; Arizzoli-Clémentel 2002, p. 152

CAT. 44 Pair of *bergères* and a
firescreen for the comtesse
Du Barry's private cabinet at the
Château de Saint-Hubert, 1770–1771

NICOLAS-QUINIBERT FOLIOT (1706–
1776), MASTER IN 1729

Wood carved by Pierre-Edme Babel (d. ca. 1779); Stamped
N.Q.FOLIOT and painted under the webbing of one of the
bergères Du N° 4285/4 and on the horizontal member of
the screen *Du N° 4285*; Painted beech; modern upholstery;
40¼ × 27 × 28 in. (1.03 m × 68.5 cm × 71 cm) (*bergères*);
43¼ × 31¼ × 17⅛ in. (1.11 m × 79.5 cm × 43.5 cm) (screen);
Inv. v 5749 1–2 and v 5756

PROVENANCE: Commissioned in 1770 and delivered in
1771 for the private cabinet of the comtesse Du Barry in
the Château de Saint-Hubert; sent to the Garde-Meuble
in 1784; supplied for use of the princess de Lamballe at
Fontainebleau; *bergères* acquired by the Versailles Foundation in 1994 (Christie's New York, October 26, 1994,
lot 148); firescreen screen acquired in 1995 (Paris, Hôtel
Drouot, Jean-Louis Ader, April 11, 1995, lot 51)

BIBL.: Baulez 1995, 3, p. 83; Baulez 1995, 4, pp. 86–87;
Arizzoli-Clémentel 2002, pp. 224–227

EXH.: Rambouillet 2003

The Château de Saint-Hubert, a small hunting lodge in the Rambouillet forest, was built for Louis XV by the architect Ange-
Jacques Gabriel in 1755–1759. In these years, the king built several
small châteaux in the forests around Paris where he pursued his
passion for hunting: Le Butard at La Celle Saint-Cloud, Verrières,
Fausses-Reposes, La Muette in the Saint-Germain forest, Marcoussis,
and others.

These structures—many of them designed by Gabriel—were a
series of experiments in buildings with compact plans. They also
foreshadowed the Petit Trianon, albeit on an entirely different scale.
Even though it was intended only for short stays, the Château de Saint-
Hubert—the largest of these buildings—was deemed too small and
was enlarged in the 1760s with two wings for service quarters. Finally,
at the request of Madame Du Barry, it was partially refurnished.

In October 1770, a particularly ornate set of furniture was commissioned for the countess's private cabinet. It was delivered by the
upholsterer Capin on May 15, 1771. In addition to the two *bergères*
and the firescreen, the set included a sofa with three back sections,
two armchairs, and six chairs. The woodwork was by the chair maker
Nicolas-Quinibert Foliot, the decoration was carved by Pierre-Edme
Babel, and the painting in white was by the Widow Bardou. The set
was originally upholstered in blue pekin, a striped silk, painted with
branches of flowers in different colors. The pieces epitomize the *à
la grecque* style: the carving represents a very toned-down version of
the rococo and includes neoclassical or "antique" motifs such as the
interlaced pattern, acanthus leaves, and pendant husks in the seat
rail and back. Only the garlands of naturalistic flowers interspersed
with these motifs and the white painting display the simplicity appropriate for a small hunting château.

This furniture must be very similar to the set that Madame Du
Barry had commissioned from the same artisans in 1769 for the drawing room of the Petit Trianon; that furniture was also without gilding.
However, the earlier set was somewhat more extensive: it included
a settee, six armchairs, nineteen chairs—including a higher one for
the king—a firescreen, and a folding screen.

Bertrand Rondot

CAT. 44

CAT. 45 Pair of armchairs *(fauteils à la reine)*, ca. 1775

JEAN-BAPTISTE-CLAUDE SENÉ (1747–1803), MASTER IN 1769

Marks of Fontainebleau 1817 and 1833; Carved and painted beech; modern upholstery (Tassinari et Chatel, silk weavers, 1973); Inv. T 472 C

PROVENANCE: Collections of the Crown; entered the Petit Trianon in 1868

BIBL.: Williamson and Champeaux 1882, no. 124; Arizzoli-Clémentel 2002, pp. 250–251, no. 89

CAT. 46 Harp, ca. 1780

Carved, painted, and gilt wood; 63 × 33½ × 23⅝ in. (1.60 m × 85 cm × 60 cm); Inv. v 4859

PROVENANCE: Acquired by the Château de Versailles in 1972, bequest of Madame Becheau La Fonta

Marie-Antoinette was passionate about music. She had an extensive musical education in Vienna, where the young Mozart played for the royal family in 1762. Marie-Antoinette, however, preferred the composer Gluck, who was her teacher and whose work she promoted in Paris. She sang (apparently not very well), as well as played the harpsichord and her favorite instrument, the harp, which she is depicted playing in the painting by Gautier-Dagoty (fig. 28). This is not Marie-Antoinette's own harp; one of her harps is in the collection of the musée de Vendôme in France.

Pierre-Xavier Hans

The *Cabinet des glaces mouvantes* (Boudoir of Moving Mirrors)

Marie-Antoinette transformed a corner room of the château of Louis XV's time into a study (or boudoir) for her use. As the windows opened directly onto a terrace, the queen had the engineer Jean-Tobie Merklein devise mirrored shutters to give greater security and protection from prying eyes. The shutters rise out of the floor from chambers specially constructed in the basement below. This is the only room at the Petit Trianon that was entirely repaneled and decorated for Marie-Antoinette. Painted white and set against a pale blue background in the manner of Wedgwood stonewares, the panels were carved by the sculptors the Rousseau brothers in 1788. The borders are meticulously carved with miniature classical arabesques, little trophies composed of musical instruments, flowers, and cupids (fig. 19).

Figs. 47–48 Two views of the *cabinet des glaces mouvantes* (Boudoir of Moving Mirrors), showing the mirrored shutters open and closed

GEORGES JACOB (1739–1814), MASTER IN 1765

Stamped *G.JACOB* on the chair, labeled "Pavillon de Monsieur à Versailles, pour le sallon [*sic*]" (on one of the *voyeuses*); Painted walnut and beech; modern upholstery (Reboul et Fontebrune, Lyon); 37⅜ × 28⅛ × 28⅜ in. (95 × 71.6 × 72 cm) (*bergères*); 35½ × 24¼ × 27⅜ in. (90 × 61.6 × 69.6 cm) (*voyeuses*); Inv. v 4399–4406

PROVENANCE: Delivered for the Pavillon de Provence in 1785; sold in 1793; ex-collection Baron James de Rothschild, sold in Paris, December 1, 1966, lots 86–87; purchased by the Château de Versailles in 1966 through a gift of Pierre David-Weill

BIBL.: Lefuel 1923, p. 278; Robiquet 1921 (1930), pp. 1–4; Frégnac 1963, p. 232; Baulez 1981, p. 98; Arizzoli-Clémentel 2002, no. 93, pp. 259–265

The queen's close relatives wished to have, like her, private residences near the Château de Versailles to which they could retire and be free from the constraints of court life. And so they built bucolic retreats inspired by the Petit Trianon: Madame Elisabeth, the king's sister, built her Château de Montreuil in the neighborhood of the same name, at the end of the avenue de Paris; the comtesse de Provence, the king's sister-in-law, built an octagonal structure in the same area. The princes followed suit: the young comte d'Artois built Bagatelle, and the comte de Provence had a pavilion built near the Swiss lake, adjacent to the King's Kitchen Garden at Versailles.

The latter structure, erected by Jean-François Chalgrin in 1785–1786, was in fact intended for the prince's favorite, the comtesse de Balbi, who had been mistress of the robes to the comtesse de Provence since 1780. The pavilion was designed as a long, single-story building that comprised a library; a dining room; a billiard room; a round, domed salon for card-playing; a bedroom; a bathroom; and an octagonal boudoir.

An exceptional set of furniture was commissioned from Georges Jacob for the central room. The carved decoration combines "antique" motifs and naturalistically rendered garlands of flowers, suitable for a "country" house. The ornamentation was also appropriate for the furniture of a prince: bundles of oak tied with acorns, symbolizing valor, adorn the tops of the backrests. Poppies, acanthus, and bundles of knotted flowers run down the chair frames.

The furniture was delivered in two lots: in 1785, two settees, two *bergères*, two benches, six armchairs, and a firescreen, all painted in a lilac-and-white scheme; and, in 1786, two *voyeuses* (chairs for watching card games), twelve chairs, and a footstool. The carved decoration on the chairs of the latter delivery is simpler, marking a distinction between chairs meant to stay where they were placed and more easily movable chairs. All of the furniture was originally covered in silk lampas with a blue background and a large pattern of arabesques, from the Lyon firm of Reboul et Fontebrune, and characterized by the cyclops motif. The furniture now has a new fabric woven with the same motif.

Because the Pavillon de Provence was destroyed in 1798, the furniture from the salon is now displayed in the last room of the queen's apartment in the Petit Trianon, the small *cabinet des glaces mouvantes* (Boudoir of Moving Mirrors). The paneling in that room, redone in 1787 in an arabesque style by the Rousseau brothers, was painted white against a blue background, in the style of Wedgwood stoneware. The comte de Provence's furniture harmonized with the room's interior, replacing pieces that had been commissioned from Jacob by the queen's Garde-Meuble, but which have not been identified.

Bertrand Rondot

CAT. 49 Mantel clock, ca. 1780

CAT. 49 Mantel clock, ca. 1780

MICHEL-PIERRE BARANCOURT, MASTER
IN 1779; POSSIBLY FRANÇOIS RÉMOND
(1747–1812), MASTER IN 1774

Case after a model by François Vion (master founder
1764); Gilt bronze, marble; 14 × 10¼ × 5¼ in. (35.6 × 26 ×
13.3 cm); Fine Arts Museums of San Francisco, Mr. and
Mrs. E. John Magnin gift, 75.18.63

PROVENANCE: Mr. and Mrs. E. John Magnin, San Francisco, by whom bequeathed to the Fine Arts Museums of
San Francisco, 1975

BIBL.: Ottomeyer and Pröschel 1986, p. 247; Baulez 1996,
p. 28

Marie-Antoinette is known to have owned a version of this clock at the Petit Trianon. The original drawing for this model, by the sculptor Vion, names the theme as "La Douleur" (Sadness), as it depicts a woman and Cupid mourning over a dead bird that lies on the altar between them. In May 1780 the clockmaker Baran-court owed to the gilder Rémond the considerable sum of 192 *livres* (pounds) for the *dorure au mat* (matte gilding) of the model of clock known as "La Pleureuse" (The Tearful Woman), which may be the same model as this clock.[1] The high quality of the gilding on this clock by Barancourt suggests that it could indeed be the same piece.

Martin Chapman

NOTE

1. Rémond papers, Archives Nationales, Paris, 183 AQ1. With thanks to
   Patrick Leperlier for this reference.

CAT. 50 Tabletop, 1776

JEAN-HENRI RIESENER (1743–1806), MASTER IN 1768

Oak veneered with marquetry of various woods, including purplewood, tulipwood, sycamore, boxwood, and satinwood; 21⅛ × 42⅜ in. (53.5 × 108.2 cm); Victoria and Albert Museum, London, Inv. 138–1865

PROVENANCE: Marie-Antoinette, Petit Trianon; Earl of Cadogan, sold Christie's, London, April 3, 1865; South Kensington Museum, now the Victoria and Albert Museum

BIBL.: Verlet 1963, pp. 127–129; Verlet 1994, pp. 149–151; Sargentson et al., forthcoming

This shaped marquetry panel was originally the top of a table that was delivered for Marie-Antoinette's use at the Petit Trianon in 1776. The queen had taken over the corner room of the château as her study, next to her bedroom, and she needed a writing table. Made by the queen's favorite cabinetmaker, this "mechanical" table was one of Riesener's specialty pieces. Its function was diverse: it could be used for writing, reading, or dressing. For these purposes it would have a writing surface, a reading stand, and a mirror and compartments for cosmetics. Tables like this one also often contained elaborate, concealed mechanisms such as spring locks and drawers that gave the type its name.

The lavish pictorial marquetry, with its overt emblems of war and victory—the warship, globes, and trophies—may have celebrated a particular event. Although it is tempting to connect it to the American Declaration of Independence that same year, the French did not officially enter the war until 1778. As Verlet has suggested, it is an unlikely subject for a piece made for the queen. For the Petit Trianon one might have expected flowers instead (cat. 42). Already old-fashioned by this date, the warlike subject matter was more appropriate for a man, and it is possible that this panel had been made originally for Louis XV, who died two years earlier, and then was reused in a commission for the new queen. By the mid-nineteenth century this tabletop was separated from its mechanical table and set into the front flap of a new desk made in an eighteenth-century style.

Martin Chapman

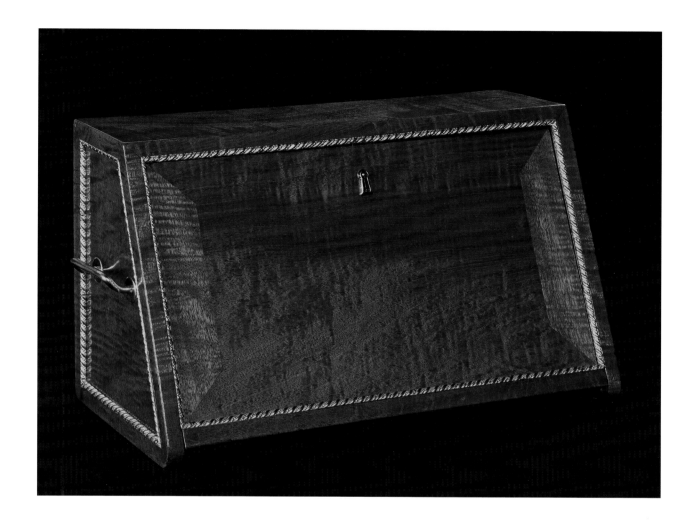

CAT. 51 Traveling desk, 1784–1789

JOSEPH GENGENBACH, CALLED CANABAS (1712–1797),
MASTER IN 1766

Stamped *Canabas*, round
mark of the Garde-Meuble
de la Reine; Mahogany
veneer; gilt-bronze mounts
and fittings; 9⅞ × 16½ ×
8 in. (25 × 42 × 20.4 cm);
Inv. v5147

PROVENANCE: Acquired by the Château de Versailles in
1978, gift of M. Jacques Perrin

BIBL.: Salverte 1934, pp. 44–45; Hans, Kobe-Tokyo, 2002,
no. 85; Hans, Bordeaux, 2005, pp. 148–149, no. 53

Fig. 49   The king's bedroom at the Petit Trianon

The King's Bedroom

The king's bedroom on the upper floor of the house was ostensibly intended for Louis XVI's use. However, he never slept at the Petit Trianon. When he visited, he dined and then returned to Versailles. The grand bed and pair of chairs were not originally made for this room, but they are upholstered in the same crimson silk patterned with Chinese motifs *à musique chinois* that was in the room during Louis XV's time.

ANTOINE-FRANÇOIS CALLET (1741–1823)

CAT. 52 *Louis XVI*, n.d.

Oil on canvas; 27½ × 22½ in. (70 × 57 cm); Inv. MV 218 and MV 7547

PROVENANCE: Mentioned at Versailles beginning in 1838, described as having an octagonal format; restored to its original oval format in 1949, at which time it was mistakenly inventoried with a new number

BIBL.: Salmon 2007, pp. 122–123 and 219, no. 39, repr. 5, no. 24

CAT. 53 Bed *(lit à la polonaise)*, ca. 1775–1785

Carved and gilded beech; modern upholstery; silk lampas *à musique chinois*; 10 ft. 4 in. × 7 ft. 2⅜ in. × 5 ft. 7⅜ in. (3.15 × 2.2 × 1.715 m); Inv. v763;

PROVENANCE: Cosson bequest, 1926

BIBL.: Arizzoli-Clémentel 2002, vol. 2, pp. 248–249, no. 88

CAT. 54 Two side chairs, 1790

JEAN-BAPTISTE-CLAUDE SENÉ (1747–1803), MASTER IN 1769

Carved and gilt walnut; modern upholstery (silk lampas *à musique chinois*); 36 × 21 × 24⅜ in. (91.5 × 53.3 × 62 cm); Inv. v5111, v5112 [only one pictured]

PROVENANCE: Louis XVI's Games Room, Château de Compiègne, 1790; purchased by the Château de Versailles in 1976

BIBL.: Verlet 1955, vol. 2, pp. 161–163, no. 40; Meyer 2002, vol. 1, pp. 172–175, no. 44; Hans, Compiègne, 2006, p. 142

Fig. 50 The queen's bedroom, known as the *chambre à coucher de treillage* (Trellis Bedroom), at the Petit Trianon

The Queen's Bedroom, or *Chambre à coucher de treillage* (Trellis Bedroom)

Made out of the former *cabinet de retraite* (retreat room) of Louis XV, later the bedroom of Madame Du Barry, this modest bedroom still has its paneling of that time. It looks out over the English gardens and the Temple of Love.

Its name, the *chambre à coucher de treillage*, derives from the trellis motif found on the clock and the wall lights (see fig. 20, now in the Calouste Gulbenkian Museum in Lisbon), which are attributed to the bronzeworker Pierre-Philippe Thomire. These bronzes, as well as the furniture, made possibly to the designs of Jean-Démosthène Dugourc, were supplied in the campaign of redecoration in 1787–1788 and executed by the queen's Garde-Meuble in the recurring rustic theme.

The seat furniture is one of the most original suites ever created, featuring naturalistically carved and painted ornament of flowers, basketwork motifs, and wheat ears, which give the suite its name, the *meuble des épis* ("wheat-ear" furniture). It was carved in minute detail after nature by the carvers Rode and then painted in lifelike colors by the artist Chaillot. The basketwork motif is reprised in the gilt-bronze mounts of the almost severe, mahogany-veneered console by Schwerdfeger. The queen's bed, which had painted trellis motifs, the armchair, and the curtains have not survived.

CAT. 55 Furniture from Marie-
Antoinette's Bedroom in the Petit
Trianon, 1787

GEORGES JACOB (1739–1814), MASTER IN
1765

Wood carved by Jean-Baptiste Rode and Jean-Baptiste-
Simon Rode; Painted by Jean-Baptiste Chaillot de Prusse;
Embroidery by Desfarges of Lyon; Painted wood; white
cotton serge (dimity), satin-stitch embroidery, and matching fine wool yarn; a. 37½ × 24¾ × 24 in. (95.3 × 63 ×
61 cm) (armchair); b. 12¼ × 18½ × 14¼ in. (31 × 47 ×
36.2 cm) (footstool); c. 43⅜ × 29⅜ × 16⅜ in. (1.113 m ×
74.5 cm × 41.5 cm) (framed firescreen); Inv. V1709, V1711,
V1714, V1713

PROVENANCE: Comissioned by Marie-Antoinette; sold in
1793; acquired by the Château de Versailles in 1942

BIBL.: Meyer 2002, pp. 274–281, no. 71; Meyer 1974,
pp. 279–80, nos. 4–5; Salverte 1975 (6th ed.), p. 166; Watson 1963, p. 137, no. 172; Gorguet-Ballesteros 2000, p. 190,
no. 108; Hans, Bordeaux 2005, no. 49

In 1786 Marie-Antoinette began to refurnish the Petit Trianon, and in the following year she commissioned a new set of furniture for her bedroom. The furniture was delivered by her personal Garde-Meuble, which was overseen by Pierre-Charles Bonnefoy du Plan. He almost certainly called upon Jean-Démosthène Dugourc to design the set.

The floral decoration of Jacob's furniture group is unique for its time. The carved wood chairs feature bundles of reeds or (possibly straw) garlanded with ivy, jasmine, lilies of the valley, and wheat ears. (The set is also known as the "wheat-ear" furniture.) Clusters of small pinecones are interspersed throughout.

What remains at Versailles of this celebrated ensemble are two armchairs, two side chairs, a firescreen, and a footstool. The J. Paul Getty Museum owns the armchair that belongs to the dressing table. The set was sold and dispersed during the Revolution; neither the Italian-style bed, also known as a "pulpit bed," nor the *bergère* has been found. Remarkably, the chairs and firescreen retain their original covers of cotton dimity embroidered in wool.

Although the archives of the queen's private Garde-Meuble have been lost, certain isolated documents identify the artisans who worked alongside Georges Jacob. The "Extrait des objets principaux employés dans l'état du Garde-Meuble des six derniers mois [de 1787]" [Account of the principal objects used in the report of the Garde-Meuble for the last six months (of 1787)] and the "Catalogue des principaux fournisseurs employés sur l'état des dépenses des six premiers mois [de] 1788" [Catalogue of the principal purveyors employed in the report of expenditures of the first six months (of) 1788] indicate that Ibert, a merchant on place du Palais Royal, provided the dimity for the entire ensemble, including the chairs, the bed, and four curtains for the windows. Desfarges, "a weaver of silk fabrics and embroiderer of Lyon," embroidered the fabric, displaying garlands of roses framing bunches of wildflowers, including buttercups and cornflowers. Triquet carved the queen's bed, and Rode carved the woodwork for the chairs and firescreen. It was "Chaillot de Prusse, Artist, who painted the wood canopy, trelliswork, jasmine, and honeysuckle, etc. of the queen's bed at Trianon in true and natural colors, as well as all the chairs."

Pierre-Xavier Hans

Detail of chair back

CAT. 56 Console table from Marie-
Antoinette's Bedroom at the Petit
Trianon, 1788

JEAN-FERDINAND-JOSEPH SCHWERDFEGER
(1734–1818), MASTER IN 1786

Signed in ink under the left drawer: *FERDINAND
SCHWERDFEGER ME.EBENISTE—A PARIS—1788*; Oak
with figured mahogany veneer; gilt bronze; veined marble
top; 33⅞ × 56¼ × 18¾ in. (86 cm × 1.43 m × 47.7 cm);
Inv. v5106

PROVENANCE: Commissioned by Marie-Antoinette; sold
in October 1793; Yusupov Collection, Saint Petersburg;
confiscated in 1917; sold by the Soviet government in
1928; Hans Rudolph Collection, Hamburg, March 21, 1952,
no. 287; Alexis de Gunzburg Collection; purchased in 1976
(Palais Galliera, Paris, November 24, 1976, no. 118)

BIBL.: Baulez 1980, p. 113, no. 92; Baulez 1990, p. 36;
Meyer 1974, pp. 279–283, nos. 4–5; Meyer 2002, pp. 282–
283, no. 72; Hans, Bordeaux, 2005, no. 50

This large console table belonged to the suite of furniture ordered by Marie-Antoinette in 1787 for her bedroom at the Petit Trianon. Like the other pieces in the room, it was probably designed by the decorator Jean-Démosthène Dugourc. Although the disappearance of the inventories of the queen's Garde-Meuble makes it impossible to identify the furniture in the Petit Trianon with certainty, we know from the *Catalogue des principaux fournisseurs employés sur l'état de dépenses des six premiers mois [de] 1788* (Catalogue of the principal purveyors employed on the accounts of expenditures of the first six months [of] 1788) that the queen's Garde-Meuble commissioned "Commodes, Consoles, Tables de Trianon" ornately decorated with gilt bronzework. The name "Sʳ Ferdinand Ebeniste à Paris" recurs several times in this document. An account dated July 7, 1788, of the gilder Mellet refers to "the matte gilding of the bronze of three different pieces of furniture, that is, a commode, a console, and a basketwork-style table." The account's description of the bronzework corresponds to that seen on the console.

The bronze decorations—the dogs' heads, the frieze of sunflowers and thistles, the extended capitals with waterlily leaves, the basketwork motifs, the ribboned reeding—are outstanding for their originality and quality. The catalogue of the principal purveyors for 1788 suggests that the bronzes were cast by Turpin and chased by Duport and Marant.

A small rectangular table also shown in the bedroom, bequeathed to the Louvre in 1914 by Baron Schlichting and placed at Trianon in 1975, is signed and dated in the same way as the console (fig. 50). The fact that the small table does not display the basketwork design indicates that Schwerdfeger made other pieces of furniture of this type for the queen beyond this bedroom suite. Marie-Antoinette also chose Schwerdfeger for her most important furnishings, such as her jewel cabinet, made in 1787 (fig. 15). His exceptional work expressed the queen's taste on the eve of the Revolution.

This console is notable for the remarkable chasing of its bronzes and its use of richly figured mahogany. Schwerdfeger's technical ability is further evident in the construction and invisible attachment of the bronzes. Here, the cabinetmaker responded to the queen's order with an extremely luxurious piece whose severe lines appear to us to be very modern.

Pierre-Xavier Hans

CAT. 57 The "Eaglets" Clock, 1787–1788

ROBERT ROBIN (1742–1799), MASTER IN 1767

PIERRE-PHILIPPE THOMIRE (1751–1843), MASTER IN 1772

Dial signed *ROBIN H^{GER} DU ROI*; Gilt bronze, enamel, glass, clockwork; 17 × 15 in. (43 × 38 cm); Inv. T 540 C

PROVENANCE: Delivered for Marie-Antoinette's bedroom in the Petit Trianon in 1788; in the Luxembourg Palace in 1796; Empress Josephine's boudoir in the Tuileries in 1807

BIBL.: Ottomeyer and Pröschel 1986, p. 240; Verlet 1987, p. 466; Ledoux-Lebard 1989, p. 173, no. 3527; Augarde 1996, p. 239; Baulez 2000, p. 104; Baulez 1996, p. 27

In the years 1787–1788 Pierre-Philippe Thomire, the queen's bronze-worker, supplied a group of bronze furnishings for the Petit Trianon that included pairs of wall lights; the "eaglets" clock, with its works by Robert Robin; and several firedogs.

The clock is composed of a trelliswork base that rests on four feet designed as baskets. The two eaglets that support the clock refer to Austria, indicating that the piece was made especially for Marie-Antoinette. The dial, signed *ROBIN H^{ger} DU ROI*, is framed with sprays of roses and other flowers. Unfortunately, the clock has been altered. It was originally flanked by a white marble Cupid holding a medallion with the queen's cipher. The 1793 inventory of Marie-Antoinette's clocks gives the following description: "A clock made up of a trelliswork base upon which is a drum borne by two eagles, within which is the clockwork under the name of Robin, next to it is a child bearing above the clock the Queen's medallion."

Inexplicably, the clock was not sold in the sales of 1793. It later graced Empress Josephine's boudoir in the Tuileries. The 1807 inventory of the Tuileries noted on the left of the dial a marble Cupid supporting a crown, which replaced the medallion with Marie-Antoinette's cipher, and on the right of the dial a basket of flowers. The white marble Cupid may have disappeared during the revolution of 1830. When the firm of Thomire restored and regilded the clock in 1837, it completed the base with the two little bouquets of flowers.

After its restoration in 1837, the clock returned to the Petit Trianon to furnish the dressing room in the apartment of the duchesse d'Orléans. It was thus reinstalled in its original surroundings.

Robert Robin, the royal clockmaker, made a great many clocks for the Crown. He worked with a number of craftsmen for the cases, notably François Rémond, Claude Galle, Balthazar Lieutaud, Etienne Levasseur, Jean-Henri Riesener, Jean-Ferdinand-Joseph Schwerdfeger, Adam Weisweiler, and Thomire. The 1793 inventory of the queen's clocks lists twenty-three with works by Robin. Marie-Antoinette shared a taste for clocks with the king, and in particular enjoyed fine gilt bronzes.

Pierre-Xavier Hans

CAT. 58 Dressing table for Marie-Antoinette's apartment at the Château des Tuileries, Paris, 1784

JEAN-HENRI RIESENER (1734–1806), MASTER IN 1768

Brand mark of the Tuileries, 2G; mark of the Tuileries under the Empire; No. 3362 Garde-Meuble de la Couronne; three labels from the late 18th century, one is: *no 7. Liste civile, toilette plaqué. Maison Egalité. Réservé* (Palais Royal); Marquetry of gray satinwood, kingwood; gilt-bronze mounts; 29⅛ × 33⅞ × 20⅞ in. (74 × 86.2 × 53 cm); Inv. T 551c

PROVENANCE: Tuileries, 1784–1792; Tuileries under the Empire; Versailles under Louis-Philippe, 1835; Garde-Meuble de la Couronne, 1863; sent to the Petit Trianon in 1867

BIBL.: Verlet 1992, pp. 93–95, no. 17; Meyer 2002, vol. 1, pp. 244–246; Hans, Bordeaux, 2005, pp. 132–133, no. 45

Gardens, Pavilions, and Follies

During Marie-Antoinette's era the grounds of the Petit Trianon were greatly transformed into pleasure gardens. Based on the advice of the comte de Caraman, the queen's architect Richard Mique, with the assistance of the painter Hubert Robert, created an English-style park with meandering streams, winding paths, and hillocks, in the manner of a natural landscape. Derived ultimately from the ideas of the philosopher Jean-Jacques Rousseau, who revered the beauty and simplicity of nature, English-style gardens came into vogue in France during this time.

The extensive park at the Petit Trianon was sprinkled with temples, follies, and pavilions, as well as the famous Hameau, the model village. From 1776 to 1783, a hectic program of building produced a variety of classical, exotic, and picturesque or "natural" structures and features, which ornamented this new landscape and provided anchoring points in the vistas.

Fig. 51 A view of the Rock and the Belvedere from the lake

MAGLOIRE THOMAS DAUSSY (ACTIVE SECOND HALF OF THE 18TH CENTURY)

CAT. 59 *Plan of the Queen's Garden at Trianon*

Signed in pen and India ink at upper left, below the cartouche enclosing the title: *Dessiné par Magloire Thomas Daussy;* Pen and gray ink, with watercolor highlights on cream-colored paper; 18½ × 29¼ in. (46.9 × 74.1 cm); Inv. VMS 90, Inv. dessins 311

PROVENANCE: Acquired by the Château de Versailles by exchange with the Musée Carnavalet, Paris, May 9, 1898

BIBL.: Hoog 1992, p. 108, no. 63, repr. p. 109; Salmon, Bordaux, 2005, pp. 171–172, no. 64, repr.

FRENCH SCHOOL, FIRST HALF OF THE 19TH CENTURY, AFTER A PLAN ATTRIBUTED TO RICHARD MIQUE (1728–1794)

CAT. 60 *Plan of the French and English Gardens at Trianon*

Inscribed: *Jardin pittoresque du petit Trianon;* Pen and India ink, with watercolor highlights on cream-colored paper; 18¼ × 25¾ in. (46.4 × 65.5 cm); Inv. MV 7281, Inv. dessins 731

PROVENANCE: Henri Grosseuvre Collection, Versailles; purchased by the Château de Versailles privately before the sale of the collection organized at the Hôtel Drouot, Paris, April 16–18, 1934

BIBL.: Hoog 1992, pp. 108 and 110, no. 64; Salmon, Bordeaux, 2005, pp. 172–173, no. 65, repr.

FRENCH SCHOOL, SECOND HALF OF THE 18TH CENTURY

CAT. 61 *The Queen's Gardens at Trianon in 1783*

Inscribed: *A Paris Chez le Rouge, Rue des Grands Augustins;* Engraving and etching on cream-colored paper; 9½ × 15¼ in. (24 × 38.6 cm); Inv. grav. 643

PROVENANCE: Old collection of the Château de Versailles

FRENCH SCHOOL, FIRST HALF OF THE 19TH CENTURY

CAT. 62 *Overall Plan of the Park and Gardens of the Two Trianons with Their Outbuildings*

Pen and watercolor on cream-colored paper; 12⅝ × 18⅛ in. (32 × 46 cm); Inv. dessins 730

PROVENANCE: Henri Grosseuvre Collection, Versailles; purchased by the Château de Versailles privately before the sale of the collection organized at the Hôtel Drouot, Paris, April 16–18, 1934

Made between the second half of the eighteenth century and the first half of the nineteenth century, these plans illustrate the changes that were made to the Trianon gardens, especially those instigated by Marie-Antoinette.

To the west, the formal garden in the French style—designed at Louis XV's request to surround the French Pavilion, the new menagerie, and the Pavillon Frais or "cool" pavilion—offered linear prospects of parterres of flowers and hedges. In 1780 Richard Mique, the queen's architect, added a small theater.

To the east, Mique designed a new garden, in an Anglo-Chinese style, between 1777 and 1781. Inspired by the gardens of the princes of Condé at Chantilly and by those of Mesdames Tantes, Louis XVI's aunts, at Bellevue, the picturesque garden combined naturalistic landscaping with fanciful buildings and follies. It included the Temple of Love, on its island, to the east; a merry-go-round; and the Belvedere, to the north. The garden was also embellished with an artificial lake, around which was built the queen's Hameau, a hamlet of houses in the style of Normandy. The complex enchanted visitors from the moment it was finished and contributed to the gardens' popularity even after the royal family left in October 1789. In 1790, the traveler Halen wrote:

> The garden, laid out in the English style, has, in keeping with today's taste, its rocks, its walks edged with stones, its hermitages, and its grottoes. But what is most beautiful of all is a charming village, of about nine houses; in the center is a green lawn bordered by a stream that one crosses by means of small, very simple bridges. The houses are rustic, it is true, but very clean and for the most part covered in climbing vines. The village lacks nothing, neither its mill, nor its tower, which is called Marlborough's Tower. Everything is well kept. But the houses the servants lived in are empty, and there are no longer heard the joyful cries that once filled the little village during the costly fêtes the Queen gave almost weekly. She has not visited her favorite place in more than a year. (Quoted by Arthur Chuquet in *Paris en 1790*, 1896)

Xavier Salmon

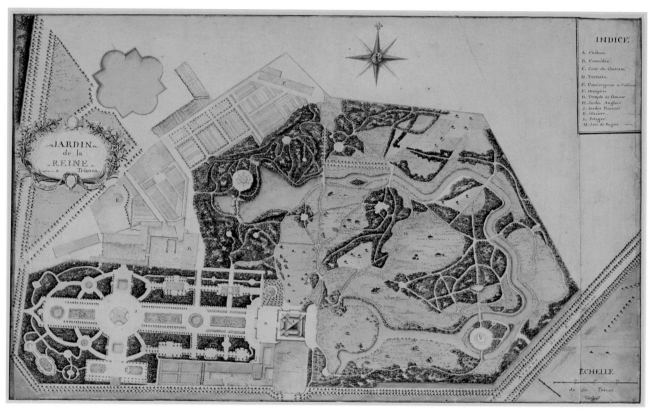

CAT. 59

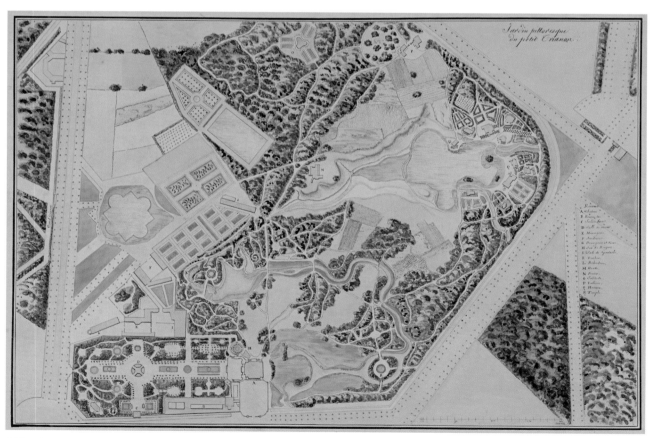

CAT. 60

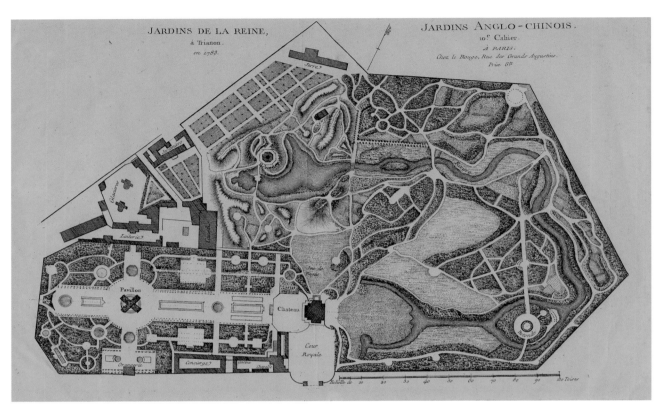

JARDINS DE LA REINE,
à Trianon.
en 1783.

JARDINS ANGLO-CHINOIS.
10.ᵉ Cahier.
À PARIS.
Chez le Rouge, Rue des Grands Augustins.
Prix 6ᵗ.

CAT. 61

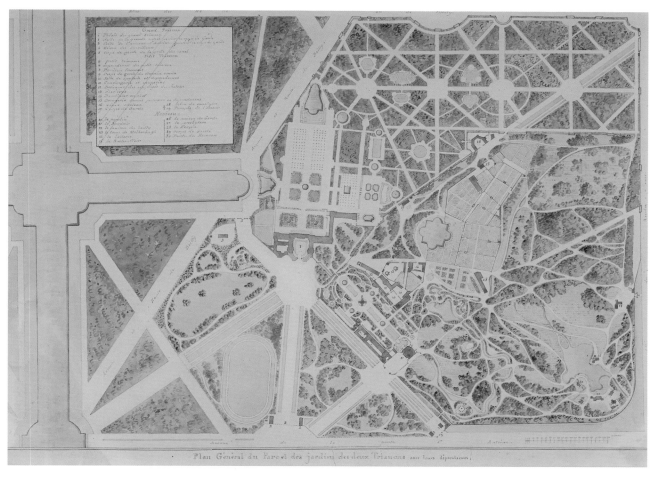

Plan Général du Parc et des jardins des deux Trianons avec leurs dépendances.

CAT. 62

RICHARD MIQUE (1728–1794) AND
CLAUDE-LOUIS CHÂTELET (1758–1795)

CAT. 63 *Souvenir Album of the Petit Trianon*, 1781

Titled: *Recueil des plans du Petit Trianon. Par le Sr. Mique Chevalier de l'ordre de St. Michel, Premier Architecte honoraire, Intendant Général des Batimens du Roy & de la Reine, 1781;* Watercolor, pen and ink, stamped morocco leather binding; 18¾ × 14¾ in. (47.5 × 37.5 cm) (size of pages); Private collection, New York

PROVENANCE: Marie-Antoinette; Count Franz Harrach, Vienna; Raphael Esmerian, Palais Galliera, Paris, June 6, 1973, Mr. and Mrs. Peter Scarisbrick, Sotheby's New York, *Fine Books and Manuscripts,* June 1, 1995, lot 303; Private collection, New York

BIBL.: *Views and Plans of the Petit Trianon* 1998

A rare document of the Petit Trianon during Marie-Antoinette's time, this album contains nine architectural plans, nine elevations, and cross sections of the Petit Trianon; as well as maps of the gardens, the French Pavilion, the Temple of Love, the Belvedere, and the Theater, all by the royal architect Richard Mique. It also contains five watercolor views by the artist Châtelet of the château, the *jeu de bague* (the merry-go-round), the Belvedere and the Rock, the Temple of Love, and the Grotto.

This album was one of at least five commissioned by Marie-Antoinette to give to her distinguished visitors. Two were presented to Gustav III of Sweden, one to Grand Duke Paul of Russia, and one to her brother Archduke Ferdinand, governor of Lombardy. This example was probably given to her brother Emperor Joseph II of Austria as a souvenir of his second visit to Versailles and the Petit Trianon, in August of 1781.

Martin Chapman

VUE du Jeu de Bague, de Sa Gallerie, & d'une des Façades du Chateau.

A. *Jeu de bague*

The Chinese-style *jeu de bague* (merry-go-round), which was built close to the château in 1776. Constructed by engineers and hand-cranked from a pit below, it had Chinese figures supporting the central pole, a dragon weathervane, and eight seats designed as dragons and peacocks. A semicircular Chinese gallery, with trellis and upswept roofs, was erected around it in 1781. It had an oval viewing room in the center.

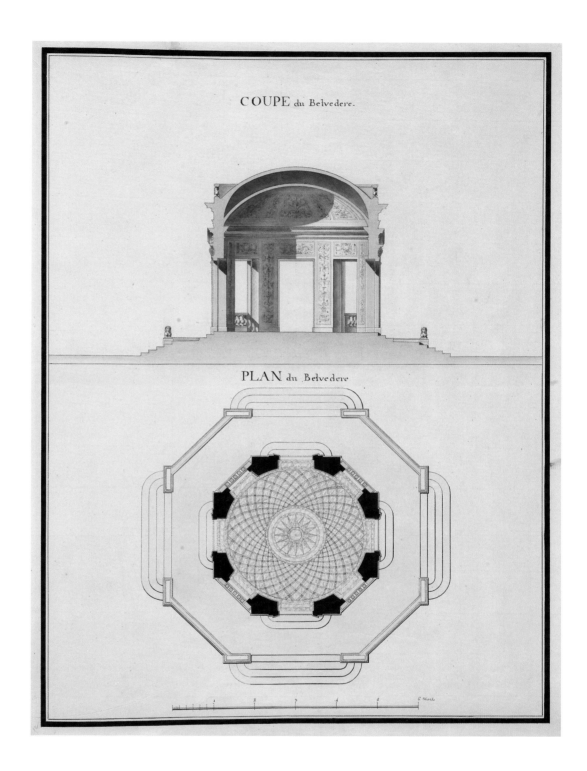

COUPE du Belvedere.

PLAN du Belvedere

B. The Belvedere

Northwest of the château is the classical Belvedere pavilion. Of octagonal form and guarded by sphinxes, it was constructed on a hill overlooking the lake to give views of the gardens. Designed by Mique in 1778 and completed in 1781, it was painted inside with arabesques on the walls. It was furnished with a suite of eight gilt-wood chairs and armchairs that were sumptuously carved by Foliot.

VUE du Belvedere et du Rocher.

VUE de l'interieur de la Grotte

C, D. The Belvedere, Rock, and Grotto

Nearby were the Rock and Grotto, which contributed a
romantic element to the gardens and provided a counter-
balance to the classicism of the Belvedere. The Grotto was
almost hidden in undergrowth and contained a chamber
decorated with moss and a waterfall. Marie-Antoinette
was in the Grotto when she received the news that the
people of Paris were marching on Versailles on October 5,
1789.

VUE du Temple.

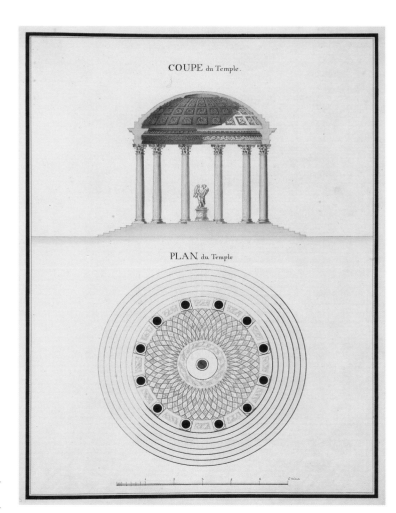

COUPE du Temple.

PLAN du Temple

E, F. The Temple of Love

The Temple of Love, built on an island in the middle of the landscaping, was visible from the eastern side of the château, where the queen's rooms were situated. Constructed in 1778 of twelve Corinthian columns (the same architectural order as the château) under a dome, it housed a copy of the sculpture by Edme Bouchardon of Cupid cutting his bow from Hercules's club. The temple was the centerpiece of the nocturnal celebrations held in honor of the visit of Marie-Antoinette's brother Joseph in 1781 and peace with England in 1782.

PLAFOND de la Salle de Spectacle.

G, H. The Theater

Built between 1778 and 1780, the Theater was sumptuously decorated with gilded ornament on a white ground
in papier-mâché and with faux-marble painting. The ornament was contrasted with light blue walls, hangings, and
upholstery. Like so many other features of the Petit Trianon, the Theater has a miniature quality, but its function
was real. In fact, it was outfitted with up-to-date, elaborate
machinery backstage. The stage was large enough to hold
full professional performances. Here the queen performed
with members of the court, in front of an invited audience.
Her last appearance was as the lowly born but beautiful
Rosina in *The Barber of Seville* by Beaumarchais.

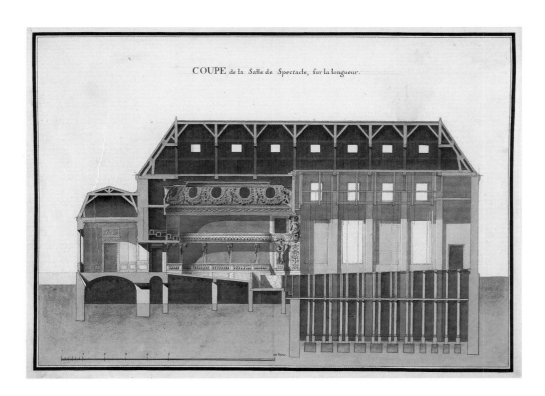

COUPE de la Salle de Spectacle, sur la longueur.

CLAUDE-LOUIS CHÂTELET (1753–1795)

CAT. 64 *Illumination of the Belvedere and of the Rock of the Petit Trianon*, 1781

Signed and dated lower left: *CHÂTELET / 1781*; Oil on canvas; 23 × 31½ in. (58.5 × 80 cm); Inv. MV 7796

PROVENANCE: Gift of Jacques Doucet to the Musée Carnavalet, Paris, in 1900; exchange with the Château de Versailles in 1949; sent to the Château de Versailles on February 17, 1950

BIBL.: de Nolhac 1927, pp. 175–176; Salmon, Bordeaux, 2005, pp. 176–177, no. 67, repr.

Marie-Antoinette gave various *fêtes* in the gardens of the Petit Trianon, beginning in 1775. Châtelet, assigned the task of documenting the property's beauty, painted several small oils of a number of the garden's structures. Today, these works constitute important illustrations of the sites and the *fêtes* during the queen's time. In 1781, the garden of the Petit Trianon was illuminated on two occasions. On July 26, the Belvedere pavilion, built in 1777, was lit up at night in honor of the comte de Provence. The effect was so successful that Marie-Antoinette decided to repeat the spectacle in early August during the visit of her brother Emperor Joseph II of Austria. Fires in earthenware pots hidden in the vegetation and bundles of firewood burning in trenches threw colors over the little buildings scattered throughout the English Garden, as well as on the trees and flowers. The Versailles painting illustrates one of these two *soirées*, though we do not know which one. The painting may have belonged to Richard Mique, who at his death owned four views of the English Garden painted by Châtelet. The queen, too, sought to preserve the memory of one of these extraordinary evenings by hanging in her apartment in the Petit Trianon Hubert Robert's very tall 1781 painting showing "an illumination given in the gardens of the New Trianon on a feast day."

Xavier Salmon

CAT. 65 Chair from the Belvedere at the Petit Trianon, 1781

JACQUES GONDOIN (1737–1818), DESIGNER

FRANÇOIS-TOUSSAINT FOLIOT (CALLED FRANÇOIS II) (1748–AFTER 1808), MASTER IN 1773

Painted on the webbing: *CT COURONNÉ* (for Château de Trianon) and *DU N° 77/8* (the queen's inventory at the Petit Trianon) and the round mark of the queen's Garde-Meuble; Carved and partially regilded beech; modern upholstery; 35½ × 22⅝ × 23 in. (90 × 57.5 × 58.5 cm); Inv. v 5358

PROVENANCE: Comissioned by Marie-Antoinette; sold in 1793; Collection Edmond de Rothschild; Aquired by the Château de Versailles as a gift in 1990

BIBL.: Baulez 1991, pp. 76–81, no. 1; Coural and Arizzoli-Clémentel 1988, pp. 53–54; Meyer 2002, pp. 229–231, no. 58; Pallot 1987, p. 41; Hans, Bordeaux, 2005, no. 44

Fig. 52 The interior of the Belvedere, completed in 1781

In 1778, Richard Mique designed the neoclassical Belvedere, an octagonal structure containing a round salon that has eight French windows. The wall decoration was completed in 1781 (fig. 52; cat. 63B). The pavilion's furniture comprised eight armchairs and eight chairs; Versailles retains only one chair of the set. The armchairs were arranged against the walls between the French windows, and the chairs were probably in a concentric circle. Jacques Gondoin, architect and designer of the royal Garde-Meuble, designed the set. His notes for the last nine months of 1780 mention the execution of a "sketch to show the queen" and especially "the models in miniature" of the armchair and chair.

Gondoin's notes also describe the wax decorations on the models, including two elements that characterize the ensemble: the ivy-wrapped torches of Hymen that form the uprights of the chair back, and the openwork rails in which a myrtle garland is wrapped around a reed. The exceptionally fine carving suggests that this was one of Marie-Antoinette's most remarkable suites of furniture, for which she called upon the most able artists and artisans. The chairs were made by the carver François II Foliot following a commission of November 29, 1780, and the assumption is that he worked with either his uncle Toussaint Foliot or Pierre-Edme Babel.

The Widow Bardou, the king's painter in ordinary, executed the gilding and the contrasting white border (no longer extant). Nau provided the original blue *gros de Tours* and lemon yellow taffeta, while the Widow Saporito furnished the very elaborate passementerie, according to an order of March 28, 1781. The frames were assigned to the upholsterer Capin, who delivered them to the royal Garde-Meuble on July 14. The item recorded as no. 4519 identifies the fabrics on the back and seat, which can be seen on the wax model as well.

Gondoin's notes record the refined and boldly colored design painted on the *gros de Tours*. The cloth displayed a pattern of small bunches of cornflowers and roses with a myrtle border. The top of each of the eight cushions was decorated with five linked crowns, one of roses and the others of laurel, which were bound together with cornflowers, the queen's favorite motif. During the Revolution, the chairs were sold as a single lot on September 4, 1793.

In addition to this chair, of the original set, four others, formerly in the collection of Baron Double (sale of May 30–June 4, 1881, lot 427), were acquired by the J. Paul Getty Museum, Los Angeles, in 1971. Unfortunately, they have lost the carving of the myrtle garland around a reed in the seat rail. Finally, one of the armchairs is in a private collection (Luigi Laura sale, Sotheby's Paris, and Poulain Lefur, June 27, 2001, lot 95).

Pierre-Xavier Hans

LOUIS-NICOLAS DE LESPINASSE, CALLED LE CHEVALIER DE LESPINASSE (1734–1808)

CAT. 66 *View of the Petit Trianon and the Temple of Love,* n.d.

Pen and gray ink, water-color, and gouache on cream-colored paper; 8½ × 13¾ in. (21.5 × 35 cm); Inv. MV8617, inv. dessins 1109

PROVENANCE: Purchased by the Château de Versailles in 1992 from Mr. Potts, Chillingham, Northumberland, through the intermediary of Mrs. Kate de Rothschild in London

BIBL.: Hoog 1992, p. 102, no. 51, repr.; Salmon 1999, p. 42, no. 33, repr. p. 43; Salmon, Bordeaux, 2005, pp. 174–175, no. 66, repr.

The Hameau

The famous Hameau was the most extensive picturesque fantasy in the gardens of the Petit Trianon. Built between 1783 and 1785, the model village originally included thatched cottages, a mill, and a dairy arranged around an artificial lake. The painter Hubert Robert was responsible for the arrangement of the structures into a painterly composition. The Queen's House, at the center, had a separate billiard room connected by a gallery. In contrast to the rustic exterior of the Queen's House, the interiors had luxurious furnishings. Beyond the hamlet was a working farm that provided the queen with eggs, butter, cream, and cheese. Swiss cattle with names like Brunette and Blanchette grazed there, and the farmer and his wife also kept ducks, hens, goats, and a pig.

Fig. 53 Marlborough's Tower of the Hameau, built in the gardens of the Petit Trianon in 1783–1785

Pierre-Joseph Wallaert (1753–1810)

CAT. 67 *The Hameau of the Petit Trianon*, 1803

Signed and dated lower left: *P. Wallaert 1803*; Oil on canvas; 22 × 28⅜ in. (56 × 72 cm); Inv. MV7125

PROVENANCE: Collection of the chevalier Emile de Tarade, Château de Belleroche, near Amboise; given to the Musée de Tours in 1873–1874, but returned at the request of the chevalier's second wife, Anne Limousin; sale Château de Belleroche, October 6–9, 1881, lot 67; Cabanis Collection, Paris; Mengin Collection, Paris; purchased from Madame Henri Mengin for the Château de Versailles in 1953

BIBL.: Benoît 2005, p. 82, no. 26, repr.

ATTRIBUTED TO CHARLES-JEAN GUÉRARD (1790–ACTIVE UNTIL 1834)

CAT. 68 *The Mill at the Hameau of Trianon*, ca. 1820–1830

Oil on wood; 21¼ × 25 in.
(54 × 63.5 cm); Inv. MV
8921

PROVENANCE: Acquired by the Château de Versailles in
1993

Salle à manger du petit Trianon.　　Versailles.　　The eating Room at the little Trianon.

J. Hill, after Jean-Claude Nattes (ca. 1765–1822)

Cat. 69 *Salle à manger du Petit Trianon, Versailles (The eating room at the little Trianon)* [The Queen's House at the Hameau], 1807

Colored aquatint; 11¾ × 15 in. (29.9 × 40.5 cm) (image); Fine Arts Museums of San Francisco, Achenbach Foundation for Graphic Arts, 1963.30.17078

Provenance: Moore S. Achenbach, gift to the Achenbach Foundation for Graphic Arts, San Francisco, 1963

Bibl.: Salmon, Bordeaux, 2005, pp. 179, 188

A. *The Queen's House*

JOHN-CLAUDE NATTES (CA. 1765–1822)

CAT. 70 Views of the Hameau at the Petit Trianon

* A. *The Queen's House*, ca. 1802

Inscribed: *The eating Room at the litle* [sic] *trianon a Versaille* [sic]; Black pencil and pen and black ink on cream-colored paper; 10 × 16⅜ in. (25.6 × 41.7 cm); Inv. MV 8141.[2] Inv. dessins 629

[not pictured]

B. *The Exterior Stairs of the Queen's House at the Hameau*, ca. 1802

Black pencil on cream-colored paper; 10⅜ × 16⅜ in. (26.3 × 41.8 cm); Inv. MV 8141.[3] Inv. dessins 630

* C. *The Guardhouse*, ca. 1802

Inscribed: *the parsonage house at the litle* [sic] *Trianon Versaille* [sic]; Black pencil and pen and black and gray ink on cream-colored paper; 10⅜ × 16¼ in. (26.4 × 41.3 cm); Inv. MV 8141.[5] Inv. dessins 632

[not pictured]

D. *The Guardhouse*, ca. 1802

Inscribed: *The second vue* [sic] *of the Parsonage house*; Black pencil and pen and black and gray ink on cream-colored paper; 16½ × 10 in. (42.1 × 25.2 cm); Inv. MV 8141.[9] Inv. dessins 636

* E. *View of the Pond and Marlborough's Tower*, ca. 1802

Inscribed: *a distant vue* [sic] *of the tower & Bath at the litle* [sic] *trianon*; Black pencil and pen and black and gray ink on cream-colored paper; 16½ × 9½ in. (42.2 × 24 cm); Inv. V 8141.[10] Inv. dessins 637

Nattes's drawings, made around 1802, provide valuable documentation of the Hameau at the Petit Trianon. The buildings, commissioned by Marie-Antoinette, were made of light materials; as a result, not all have survived. The barn and the guardhouse, for example, no longer exist. The Hameau, or hamlet, which was largely built between 1783 and 1785, contributed to the charming but naive belief that the queen enjoyed playing at peasant and shepherdess. A deeper knowledge about the site and its uses suggests other inferences.

In 1783, Marie-Antoinette asked the architect Richard Mique, the painter Claude-Louis Châtelet, and the model-maker Freret for plans, landscape sketches, and models of a complex of cottages in the style of Normandy. She was following the aristocratic fashion for building picturesque hamlets as part of larger estates. Marie-Antoinette's Hameau was located in the north part of her Anglo-Chinese garden. Sited around an ornamental lake, on a piece of land surrounded by a moat, the houses were arranged into two groups separated by a small river. On one side were the mill, the boudoir, and the Queen's House, with its servants' quarters in the back; on the other side were houses for the guard and gardener, the barn, the henhouse, and Marlborough's Tower with its outbuildings, including the dairy and the fishery. Further away was the farm.

Construction began in earnest in 1784, after the necessary landscaping, which consisted of laying out the paths and digging the lakes and rivers. The exterior walls of the buildings were painted and decorated *en vétusté*—in a "decrepit style"—with the intentional effects of old bricks, weathered stone, artificial cracks, and ruined plaster. The roofs of all the buildings were thatched, except for those of the Queen's House and the dairy, which were tiled.

In 1787 most of the work was finished, and the queen could fully enjoy her new Hameau. The little buildings of the hamlet housed two kinds of activities: those relating to court life and those typical of farm life. Five houses were reserved for the use of Marie-Antoinette

Fig. 54 The Queen's House

C. *The Guardhouse*

E. *View of the Pond and Marlborough's Tower*

F. *Marlborough's Tower*

* F. *Marlborough's Tower,* ca. 1802

Inscribed: *The tower at the little trianon;* Black pencil and pen and black and gray ink on cream-colored paper; 16½ × 10½ in. (42 × 26.6 cm); Inv. MV 8141.[13] Inv. dessins 640

[not pictured]

G. *The Mill,* ca. 1802

Inscribed: *mill at the litle* [sic] *trianon;* Black pencil and pen and black and gray ink on cream-colored paper; 10⅛ × 16½ in. (25.7 × 42.1 cm); Inv. MV 8141.[6] Inv. dessins 633

* H. *Second View of the Mill,* ca. 1802

Inscribed: *a second vue* [sic] *of the mill;* Black pencil and pen and black and gray ink on cream-colored paper; 16½ × 9¾ in. (42 × 24.7 cm); Inv. MV 8141.[7] Inv. dessins 634

[not pictured]

I. *Third View of the Mill,* ca. 1802

Inscribed: *the third vue* [sic] *of the mill;* Black pencil and pen and black and gray ink on cream-colored paper; 16¾ × 9⅞ in. (42.4 × 25.1 cm); Inv. MV 8141.[8] Inv. dessins 635

[not pictured]

J. *The Boudoir,* ca. 1802

Inscribed: *le boudoir du petit trianon favorite place / of the late Queen of France* and in pencil *roud* and *The sashes of the / windows perfect / each step one stone neatly cut / stone under the windows new;* Black pencil and pen and black and gray ink on cream-colored paper; 16¾ × 10¼ in. (42.4 × 26 cm); Inv. MV 8141.[11] Inv. dessins 638

[not pictured]

K. *The Barn,* ca. 1802

Inscribed: *the B*[e struck through]*arn of the litle* [sic] *trianon;* Black pencil and pen and black and gray ink on cream-colored paper; 16½× 10½ in. (42.1 × 26.7 cm); Inv. MV 8141.12 Inv. dessins 639

and her guests. The Queen's House and the adjacent structure, which contained a billiard room, displayed particularly well-finished interiors. The dining room, backgammon room, Chinese parlor, and billiard room allowed the social life of the Petit Trianon to be replicated for smaller parties. Nearby, the boudoir and warming room, with its kitchen, bakehouse, woodshed, pantry, linen room, silver room, and scullery, as well as a house for the footmen, assured impeccable service. The peasant activities were assigned to the farm, which was far enough away to spare the queen and her guests the smells of the cows, goats, and pigs; the farm also included the barn, the dovecote—also known as the henhouse—and the working dairy. These places allowed the farmer, Valy Bussard, and his assistants to run a genuine agricultural enterprise that included plowing fields, cultivating

Fig. 55 Marlborough's Tower

H. *Second View of the Mill*

[not pictured]

L. *Four sketches of the Boudoir of the Hameau of the Petit Trianon (Three Exterior Views and One Interior View of the Kitchen),* ca. 1802

Black pencil and pen and black ink on cream-colored paper; 10½ × 16½ in. (26.5 × 42 cm); Inv. MV 8141.[1] Inv. dessins 628

PROVENANCE: From a group of fifteen sheets (Inv. MV 141[1–15], Inv. dessins 628–42) offered to the Château de Versailles in 1960 by the Société des Amis de Versailles; executed by Nattes around 1802 as preparatory works for a collection of engravings to be included in *La capitale de la France et ses environs avec une description,* in-folio, seventy-nine pages, published by William Miller in London and illustrated with forty aquatints etched between 1805 and late 1810 by J. Hill; purchased by the Château de Versailles from the Paris bookseller Roux Devillas

BIBL.: Hoog 1992, pp. 102–105, nos. 52–60, repr.; Salmon, Bordeaux, 2005, pp. 178–190, nos. 68–78, repr.

the gardens that Antoine Richard had designed around the houses, felling trees, harvesting and gathering fruit, and raising cows, sheep, goats, pigs, rabbits, and hens.

The Hameau's simplicity gave the country life an overtone of "exoticism." It satisfied the queen's desire to escape the burdensome constraints of the court's etiquette. But the flimsily built Hameau required constant upkeep. The years of the Revolution and the subsequent abandonment of the buildings were particularly damaging. In the Empire period, some of the structures were in such poor condition that they were torn down. Yet, even in their dilapidated state, the surviving buildings remained objects of curiosity and wonder, as demonstrated by these drawings by Nattes, which were to be published as aquatints (cat. 69).

Xavier Salmon

Fig. 56 The Mill

Versailles. Le Village Suisse. Maison du Seigneur

JULES HAUTECOEUR (ACTIVE 19TH CENTURY), PUBLISHER

CAT. 71 *Versailles, Le Village Suisse, Maison de Seigneur* [The Queen's House at the Hameau, Versailles], ca. 1900

Albumen silver print; 7⅛ × 9¹³⁄₁₆ in. (18.2 × 24.9 cm) (image); Fine Arts Museums of San Francisco, gift of Serge Millan, 1988.3.8

PROVENANCE: Serge Millan, gift to the Achenbach Foundation for Graphic Arts, San Francisco, 1988

BIBL.: Hautecoeur ca. 1900

CAT. 72 Sideboard, ca. 1785

JEAN-HENRI RIESENER (1734–1806),
MASTER IN 1768

Brand marks of the Petit Trianon (crowned *CT*) and the
queen's Garde-Meuble, and a number painted in ink:
DU Nº 78.1; Oak, mahogany, and mahogany veneer; top
of veined white marble; gilt bronze; 31¾ × 71 × 21½ in.
(80.5 cm × 1.802 m × 54.5 cm); Inv. v 4783

PROVENANCE: Commissioned by Marie-Antoinette for
the dining room of the Petit Trianon; sold in 1793; purchased by the Château de Versailles in 1971

BIBL.: Meyer 1974, p. 282; Meyer 2002, pp. 290–291

The interiors of the picturesque and rustic houses of the Hameau,
in contrast to the facades, were luxurious. These buildings, in
particular the Queen's House, located in the middle of the hamlet,
were meant to receive the queen and her guests. The Queen's House
comprises two structures that are connected by a wooden gallery
reached by a spiral staircase. The house is roofed with tiles, not
thatch like the other buildings. On the ground floor is a vast dining
room, and the floor above has an anteroom for nobles, a salon, and
a small backgammon room. The adjacent structure houses a billiard
room on the ground floor and a series of small rooms above, including a Chinese parlor.

Almost all the furniture for the Hameau was commissioned
through the queen's private Garde-Meuble. The orders appear to
have been filled solely by Georges Jacob (for the chairs) and Jean-
Henri Riesener (for the cabinetry). As the archives of the queen's
Garde-Meuble have disappeared, scholars have relied on identifying
marks and numbers, especially on the dining-room pieces, to recon-
struct the furniture's history.

In addition to the marks of the Petit Trianon and the queen's
Garde-Meuble, the number 78, corresponding to a room in the inventory of the Petit Trianon property, made it possible to reassemble a
set of furniture from a dining room. Too simple for the château, the
set must have come from the Queen's House in the Hameau; the
records of the Revolutionary-era sales confirm this designation.

CAT. 73 Corner cupboard, ca. 1785

JEAN-HENRI RIESENER (1734–1806),
MASTER IN 1768

Stamped *J.H. RIESENER,* branded marks of the Petit Trianon (crowned *CT*) and the queen's Garde-Meuble, and a
number painted: *DU N⁰ 78.2;* Oak, mahogany, and mahogany veneer; top of veined white marble; gilt bronze; 35 ×
20 × 14⅛ in. (89 × 51 × 36 cm); Inv. v 3795

PROVENANCE: Commissioned by Marie-Antoinette for the
dining room of the Petit Trianon; sold in 1793; purchased
by the Château de Versailles in 1962 (sale Paris, Palais Galliera, Me Ader, April 11, 1962, lot 146)

BIBL.: Meyer 1974, p. 282, fig. 4; Meyer 2002,
pp. 290–291

The mahogany sideboard features the dining room's most
significant aesthetic statement. Designed for serving food, it has
a main drawer, two side drawers that swing open, and two ample
marble surfaces. With their simple moldings, the corner cupboard
and its mate—the existence of the latter is proved by the number
78.2, which indicates that two identical pieces of furniture were
delivered—adorned two corners of the room, and probably each
supported a candelabrum. Similarly, the identifying mark indicates
how many chairs Jacob delivered: twenty mahogany lyre-back chairs,
covered in green morocco leather, some checked, the others solid. Of
these, the museum at Versailles has been able to collect eight. Only
the mahogany dining table has not yet been located.

As at the main château of the Petit Trianon, the dining-room
furniture at the Hameau had to be both elegant and practical. In
contrast to traditional chairs made of painted wood, these chairs
were made of fashionable mahogany, which was prized for its dark
tones, recalling the patina of ancient bronze, and for its fine grain,
which allowed for additional delicacy. The lyre motif, a reference

CAT. 74 Two chairs, ca. 1785

GEORGES JACOB (1739–1814), MASTER IN
1765

Mark and number painted on the webbing: crowned *CT*
and *DU N° 78./20*; Mahogany; 35½ × 18½ × 18½ in. (90 ×
47 × 47 cm); Inv. V5808 1–2 [only one pictured]

PROVENANCE: Commissioned by Marie-Antoinette for
the dining room of the Petit Trianon; sold in 1793; purchased by the Château de Versailles in 1997 (sale Paris,
Hôtel Drouot, Me Millon, April 2, 1997, lot 146)

BIBL.: Baulez 1997 (2) 5–6, p. 117; Baulez 1999, pp. 30–31;
Meyer 2002, pp. 290–291

EXH.: Bordeaux, 2005, no. 47

to antiquity, and the use of mahogany attest to the period's reign-
ing Anglomania, a fashion for all things English that swept France
in the early 1780s. Georges Jacob introduced into French furniture
the typical English-style chair back formed by a fretted splat, which
until then had been unknown in France, where upholstered or caned
backs were favored.

The salon upstairs was more richly furnished, with four corner
cupboards by Riesener, which are now in the collections of the Art
Institute of Chicago and the Saint Louis Art Museum.

These refined, yet unostentatious, pieces are typical of Marie-
Antoinette's taste in decoration for the Hameau, where she hoped to
retreat from her royal position. Her pursuit of a stylish life, removed
from the pomp of the court, is confirmed by accounts like this one,
from Boulard, the queen's former *valet de chambre,* in 1809: "The furniture of the Petit Trianon was all elegant, but extremely simple." The
phrase applies equally to the dining-room furniture at the Hameau.

Bertrand Rondot

CAT. 75 Pair of firedogs, ca. 1785

ATTRIBUTED TO PIERRE-PHILIPPE
THOMIRE (1751–1843), MASTER IN 1772

Gilt bronze, enamel; Height 19 in. (48.3 cm); Museum
of Fine Arts, Boston, Bequest of Miss Elizabeth Howard
Bartol, 27.521.1

PROVENANCE: Dining Room of the Queen's House at the
Hameau, Petit Trianon; sale September 30, 1793, lot 2354,
for 4775 *livres* to the dealer Rocheux, Paris; probably bought
in Paris 1794/5 by James Swan, Boston; by inheritance to
Mrs. John C. Howard; by inheritance to Miss Elizabeth
Howard Bartol, who bequeathed them to the Museum of
Fine Arts, Boston, September 1927

BIBL.: Verlet 1987, p. 44; Salmon, Bordeaux, 2005,
pp. 68–78

Each designed as a pair of goats eating grapes, these firedogs are emblems of the classical mythology of Bacchus. Such imagery was often used in the eighteenth century for objects associated with dining and drinking, and appropriately these firedogs were probably supplied for the dining room of the Queen's House at the Hameau.[1] Because the interiors at the Hameau deteriorated quickly after the Revolution—little is known about their original decorative schemes. We know that some of the furniture was very plain, in keeping with the simple and rustic aesthetic of the Hameau. It also reflected the fashion for Anglomania in the 1780s (see cats. 72–74). In contrast, these meticulously modeled firedogs, executed in expensive gilt bronze, show just how rich some of the furnishings at the Hameau could be, especially objects intended for the queen's use. However simple the furniture was, somehow restrained richness was never far away in the queen's schemes of decoration. The firedogs are attributed to Thomire who was one of the ablest bronze workers supplying fireplace fittings and lighting (including the famous Trianon lantern) for the royal châteaux around 1785.

The Boston merchant James Swan acquired many pieces of French royal furniture at the time of the Revolutionary sales of the royal palaces. He probably owned these firedogs shortly after the sale of the contents of the Petit Trianon and the Hameau in August and September 1793, in which they were sold to the dealer Rocheux for 4775 *livres*. Swan was the agent for the French government to acquire supplies of food and war materials in America in exchange for luxury goods; and this may have been the case with these firedogs.

Martin Chapman

NOTE

1. Bill for cleaning in files at the Museum of Fine Arts, Boston, from Patrick Leperlier: "Mémoire des objets de nettoyage et racommodage faits tant à Trianon, qu'au château et Hameau pendant les mois de May et Juin 1788. Nettoyage du Hameau. . . . le feu à bouc et la balustrade de la salle à manger. 6 livres." (Bill for cleaning and furbishing objects at Trianon, either at the château or at the Hameau in the months of May and June 1788. Hameau cleaning. . . . The goat firedogs and balustrade from the dining room, 6 pounds.)

Bibliography

Alcouffe, Daniel, Anne Dion-Tenenbaum, and Amaury Lefébure. *Le mobilier du musée du Louvre.* Vol. 1. Dijon, 1993.

Arizzoli-Clémentel, Pierre. *Le mobilier de Versailles, XVIIème et XVIIIème siècle.* Vol. 2. Dijon, 2002.

Augarde, J.-D. *Les Ouvriers du temps,* 1996.

Baillio, Joseph. *Elisabeth Louise Vigée Le Brun 1755–1842.* Fort Worth: Kimbell Art Museum, 1982.

Baulez, Christian. "Jean-Ferdinand-Joseph Schwerdfeger. Console." In *Cinq années d'enrichissement du patrimoine national, 1975–1980.* Paris, 1980.

———. "Meubles royaux récemment acquis à Versailles (1985–1989)." *Revue du Louvre* (1990): no. 2, pp. 94–106.

———. "Deux sièges de Foliot et de Séné pour Versailles." *Revue du Louvre* (1991): no. 1, pp. 76–81.

———. "Versailles, vers un retour de Sèvres." *Revue du Louvre* (1991): nos. 5–6, pp. 62–76.

———. "Acquisitions." *Revue du Louvre* (1994): no. 1, p. 94.

———. "Acquisitions." *Revue du Louvre* (1994): no. 3, pp. 78–79, 92.

———. "Acquisitions." *Revue du Louvre* (1995): no. 3, p. 83.

———. "Acquisitions." *Revue du Louvre* (1995): no. 4, pp. 86–87.

———. *The Petit Trianon and the Queen's Hamlet, Visitor's Guide.* Versailles: Editions Art Lys, 1996.

———. "Acquisitions." *Revue du Louvre* (1997): nos. 5–6, p. 117.

———. "Acquisitions." *Revue du Louvre* (1998): no. 3, p. 92.

———. "Huit chaises pour la salle à manger de Marie-Antoinette au Hameau de Trianon." *Versalia* 2 (1999): pp. 30–31.

———. "Le grand cabinet intérieur de Marie-Antoinette, Décor, mobilier et collections." In *Les Laques du Japon: Collections de Marie-Antoinette.* Versailles: Château de Versailles; Münster: Museum für Lackkunst, 2001.

Baumstark, Reinhold, and Helmut Seling. *Silber und Gold Augsburger Goldschmiedekunst für die Höfe Europas.* Munich: Bayerisches National Museum, 1994.

Benoit, Jérémie. *Napoléon et Versailles.* Versailles: Château de Versailles, 2005.

Bourgeois, Emile. "L'état civil des bustes et médallions de Marie-Antoinette et de Louis XVI." *La Revue de l'art ancien et moderne* 22 (July–Dec. 1907): pp. 401–412.

Boysson, Bernadette de, and Xavier Salmon. *Marie-Antoinette à Versailles: Le goût d'une reine.* Paris: Somogy éditions d'art; Bordeaux: Musée des arts décoratifs, 2005.

Brière-Misme, Clotilde. "La résurrection de la salle à manger de Louis XV au Petit Trianon." *Bulletin de la Société d'histoire de l'art français* (1967). Paris, 1968, pp. 217–240.

[Bordeaux]. Boysson, Bernadette de, and Xavier Salmon. *Marie-Antoinette à Versailles: Le goût d'une reine.* Paris: Somogy éditions d'art; Bordeaux: Musée des arts décoratifs, 2005.

Campardon, Emile. *Marie-Antoinette à la conciergerie (du 1er Août au 16 octobre 1793), Pièces originales conservées aux Archives de l'Empire suivies de notes historiques et du procès imprimé de la reine.* Paris: J. Gay, 1863.

Champeaux, Alfred de, and Edouard-Thomas Williamson. *Catalogue des objets appartenant au Service du Mobilier National: exposition rétrospective de 1882.* Union Centrale des Arts Décoratifs, ed. Paris: A. Quantin, 1882.

Coural, Chantal, and Pierre Arizzoli-Clémentel. *Soieries de Lyon, Commandes royales au XVIIIème siècle (1730–1800).* Lyon: Musée historique des Tissus, 1988.

De Bellaigue, Geoffrey. *The James A. de Rothschild Collection at Waddesdon Manor. Furniture, Clocks, and Gilt Bronzes.* 2 vols. London: The National Trust, 1974.

Desjardins, Gustave. *Le Petit Trianon. Histoire et description.* Paris, 1885.

Draper, James David, and Guilhem Scherf. *Augustin Pajou, Royal Sculptor, 1730–1809.* New York: Metropolitan Museum of Art, 1997.

Engerand, Fernand. *Inventaire des tableaux commandés et achetés par la direction des Bâtiments du Roi (1709–1792).* Paris, 1900.

Frégnac, Claude. *Les ébénistes du XVIIIe siècle français.* Paris: Hachette, 1963.

Gabillot, C. "Les trois Drouais (Troisième article). François-Hubert Drouais (1727–1775)." *Gazette des Beaux-Arts* (1906): no. 1, pp. 155–174.

Gorguet-Ballesteros, Pascal. *Le coton et la mode, 1000 ans d'aventures.* Paris: Musée Galliéra, 2000.

Hans, Pierre-Xavier. In [Bordeaux]. Boysson, Bernadette de, and Xavier Salmon. *Marie-Antoinette à Versailles: Le goût d'une reine.* Paris: Somogy éditions d'art; Bordeaux: Musée des arts décoratifs, 2005.

———. In [Compiègne]. *Louis XVI et Marie-Antoinette à Compiègne.* Paris: Réunion des Musées Nationaux, 2006.

Hautecoeur, Jules, ed. *Paris, St. Cloud, Versailles & Trianons, 50 photogravures.* Paris, ca. 1900.

Havard, Henry. *Dictionnaire de l'ameublement et de la décoration depuis le XIIIe siècle jusqu'à nos jours.* Vol. 4 (4 Vols.). Paris: Ancienne maison Quentin, n.d.

Herdt, Anne de, and Lydie de La Rochefoucauld. *Louis-Auguste Brun 1758–1815 dit Brun de Versoix. Catalogue des peintures et dessins.* Geneva, 1986.

Hoog, Simone. In *Les jardins de Versailles et de Trianon d'André le Nôtre à Richard Mique.* Versailles: Château de Versailles, 1992.

———. *Musée national du château de Versailles. Les sculptures. I. Le musée.* Paris, 1993.

Jallut, Marguerite. *Marie-Antoinette et ses peintres.* Paris, 1955.

———. "Château de Versailles. Cabinets intérieurs et petits appartements de Marie-Antoinette." *Gazette des Beaux-Arts* (May 1964): pp. 300–310.

[Kobe-Tokyo]. *Fastes de Versailles.* Kobe-Tokyo: Municipal Museum, 2002.

Kopplin, Monika, and Christian Baulez. *Les laques du Japon: Collections de Marie-Antoinette.* Versailles: Château de Versailles; Münster: Museum für Lackkunst, 2001.

Ledoux-Lebard, Denise. *Versailles: Le Petit Trianon, Le mobilier des inventaires de 1807, 1810 et 1839.* Paris: Editions de l'amateur, 1989.

Lefuel, Hector. *Georges Jacob et les ébénistes du XVIIIe siècle.* Paris: Editions Albert Morancé, 1923.

Madame Du Barry: De Versailles à Louveciennes. Paris, 1992.

Meyer, Daniel. "A propos du mobilier de Marie-Antoinette au Petit Trianon." *Revue du Louvre* (1974): nos. 4–5, pp. 279–283.

———. "L'ameublement des petits appartements de la reine à Versailles sous Louis-Philippe." Mélanges Verlet III, *Antologia di Belle-Arti.* Nos. 31–32. Turin, 1987, pp. 28–49.

———. *Le mobilier de Versailles, XVIIème et XVIIIème siècles.* Vol. 1. Dijon, 2002.

Morel, Bernard. *The French Crown Jewels.* Antwerp: Fonds Mercator, 1988.

Nagashima, Meiko. "Edo-jidai chuki no yushutsu shikki. Marie-Antoinette no korekushon o shushin ni" ("Mid-Edo period Japanese export lacquer. The collection of Marie-Antoinette"). In *Shikkoshi* 22 (1999): pp. 25–66 and IV–V.

Nolhac, Pierre de. *Versailles et la cour de France. Trianon.* Paris, 1927.

Ottomeyer, Hans, and Peter Pröschel. *Vergoldete Bronzen.* Munich: Klinkhardt and Biermann, 1986.

Pallot, Bill G. B. *L'art du siège au XVIIIème siècle en France.* Paris, 1987.

Parker, James. *The Wrightsman Galleries at the Metropolitan Museum.* New York: Metropolitan Museum of Art, 1979.

Picquenard, Thérèse. "Les bustes de Louis-Simon Boizot sous l'Ancien Régime, portraits d'apparat et portraits intimes." *Augustin Pajou et ses contemporains.* Paris: Actes du colloque—Musée du Louvre, 1997.

———. "Les bustes de Louis-Simon Boizot sous l'Ancien Régime, portraits d'apparat et portraits intimes." *Augustin Pajou et ses contemporains.* Paris: La documentation Française—Musée du Louvre, 1999.

———. In *Louis-Simon Boizot (1743–1809). Sculpteur du roi et directeur de l'atelier de sculpture à la manufacture de Sèvres.* Versailles: Musée Lambinet, 2001.

Plinval de Guillebon, Régine de. *Faïence et porcelaine de Paris, XVIII–XIXème siècle.* 1995.

Portalis, Roger, and Henri Beraldi. *Les graveurs du dix-huitième siècle.* Paris: Damascène, Morgand et Charles Fatout, 1880.

Pradère, Alexandre. *Les ébénistes français de Louis XIV à la Révolution.* Paris; Le Chêne, 1989.

Ribero, Aileen. *The Art of Dress: Fashion in England and France 1750–1820.* New Haven: Yale University Press, 1995.

Rieder, William. "French Furniture of the Ancien Régime." *Apollo* 111 (Feb.–Mar. 1980).

Robiquet, Jacques. *Gouthière: Sa vie—son œuvre.* Paris: Henri Laurens, 1912.

———. "La propriété de la comtesse de Balbi et du comte de Provence à Versailles." *Revue de l'Histoire de Versailles* (1921 [1930]): pp. 1–14.

Salmon, Xavier. In *Versailles. Retratos de una sociedad. S. XVII–XIX.* Barcelona: Fundación La Caixa, 1993–1994.

———. *Château de Versailles. Nouvelles acquisitions du cabinet des dessins 1988–1998.* Baume-les-Dames, 1999.

———. *Trésors cachés. Chefs-d'œuvre du cabinet d'Arts graphiques du château de Versailles.* Rouen: Musée des beaux-arts; Le Mans: Musée de Tessé, 2001.

———. In [Kobe-Tokyo]. *Fastes de Versailles.* Kobe-Tokyo: Municipal Museum, 2002.

———. In [Bordeaux]. Boysson, Bernadette de, and Xavier Salmon. *Marie-Antoinette à Versailles: Le goût d'une reine.* Paris: Somogy éditions d'art; Bordeaux: Musée des arts décoratifs, 2005.

———. *Marie-Antoinette. Images d'un destin.* Neuilly-sur-Seine, 2005.

———. *Imagens do Soberano. Acervo do Palácio de Versalhes.* São Paulo: Pinacoteca do Estado, 2007.

Salverte, François de. *Les Ebénistes du XVIIIème siècle.* Paris, 1934, 1975 (first edition, 1923).

Sargentson, Carolyn, et al. *Catalogue of French Furniture 1640–1800 in the Victoria and Albert Museum.* London: V&A, forthcoming.

Scherf, Guilhem. "Jean-Baptiste Nini et le portrait sculpté en medallion au XVIIIème siècle." In *Jean-Baptiste Nini 1717–1786. D'Urbino aux rives de la Loire. Paysages et visages européens.* Milan, 2001.

Sheriff, Mary D. "Portrait of the Queen." In *Marie Antoinette, Writings on the Body of a Queen.* New York: Routledge, 2003.

Vandalle, Claude. In *Fastes de Versailles.* Kobe-Tokyo: Municipal Museum, 2002.

Verlet, Pierre. *Les Bronzes dorés français du XVIIIème siècle.* Paris: Picard, 1987.

———. *French Royal Furniture.* London: Barrie and Rockliff, 1963.

———. *Le Mobilier royal français. Meubles de la Couronne conserves en France.* Vol. 1. Paris, 1945.

———. *Le Mobilier royal français,* Vol. 2. Paris, 1955.

———. *Le Mobilier royal français.* Vol. 3. Paris, 1994.

———. *Le Mobilier royal français.* Vol. 4. Paris, 1990.

Views and Plans of the Petit Trianon at Versailles. Paris: Alain de Gourcuff, 1998.

Vigée Le Brun, Elisabeth Louise. *Souvenirs de Madame Louise Elisabeth Vigée Le Brun.* 3 vols. Paris, 1835–1837.

———. *Souvenirs.* Claudine Herrmann, ed. Paris, 1986.

Watson, Francis J. B. *Le Meuble Louis XVI.* Paris, 1963.

Weber, Caroline. *Queen of Fashion: What Marie Antoinette Wore to the Revolution.* New York: Henry Holt and Company, 2006.

Williamson, Edouard-Thomas, and Alfred de Champeaux. *Catalogue des objets appartenant au Service du Mobilier National: Exposition rétrospective de 1882.* Union Centrale des Arts Décoratifs, ed. Paris: A. Quantin, 1882.

Wine, Humphrey. In *Madame de Pompadour et les arts.* Versailles: Château de Versailles, 2002.

July 2010
10—

Acknowledgments

Photograph Credits

We would like to thank the following for their help with this catalogue and with the exhibition:

Tracey Albainy, Senior Curator of Decorative Arts and Sculpture, Art of Europe Department, Museum of Fine Arts, Boston

Dr. Colin Bailey, Chief Curator, Frick Collection, New York

Joseph Baillio, New York

Brian Considine, Head of Decorative Arts and Sculpture Conservation, J. Paul Getty Museum, Los Angeles

Charissa Bremer David, Associate Curator of Decorative Arts, J. Paul Getty Museum, Los Angeles

Ralph Esmerian, New York

Jay Gam, Getty Research Institute, Los Angeles

Louis Marchesano, Getty Research Institute, Los Angeles

Melinda McCurdy, Curator, The Huntington Art Collections, San Marino, California

Lee Hunt Miller, San Francisco

Dr. Markus Miller, Director, Hessische Hausstiftung, Museum Schloss Fasanerie, Germany

Christine Nguyen, Getty Research Institute, Los Angeles

Fern Prosnitz, San Francisco

Dr. Carolyn Sargentson, Head of Research, Victoria and Albert Museum, London

Rosalind Savill, Director, The Wallace Collection, London

George Shackelford, Chairman and Arthur K. Solomon Curator of Modern Art, Art of Europe Department, Museum of Fine Arts, Boston

Dr. Eleanor Tollfree, Curator, The Wallace Collection, London

Nuno Vassallo e Silva, Deputy Director, Museu Calouste Gulbenkian, Lisbon

Christopher Wilk, Curator of Furniture and Textiles, Victoria and Albert Museum, London

Gillian Wilson, Curator Emeritus, J. Paul Getty Museum, Los Angeles